ATLAS

OF

geographical curiosities

VITALI VITALIEV

JONGLEZ PUBLISHING

Content

Definitions

- An **exclave** is a territory under the sovereignty of a country but separated from the main territory of that country by one or several other countries or seas. Nakhichevan is therefore an exclave of Azerbaijan: it can be reached from Azerbaijan through Armenia or Iran (see page 115).

- An **enclave** is a territory completely surrounded by one other territorial entity (region or country). There are therefore three countries in the world enclaved in other countries: Vatican City and San Marino enclaved in Italy, and Lesotho, enclaved in South Africa.

- A **semi-enclave** or **semi-exclave** is an enclaved territory with access to international waters, signifying it is not completely enclaved within another territory. Monaco, The Gambia and Brunei (independent countries) are semi-enclaves, while Kalingrad (a region of Russia) is a semi-exclave – not a semi-enclave – because it is not an independent territory.

- A **pene-exclave** is a territory of a country that can only be accessed by road through another country. The Northwest Angle (USA, see page 15), Point Roberts (USA, see page 17), and Kleinwalsertal (Austria, see page 51) are examples of pene-exclaves, also referred to as 'practical' exclaves.

- A **counter-enclave** is an enclave within an enclave. There are two in the world: in Baarle (The Netherlands/Belgium, see page 57) and in Nahwa (United Arab Emirates/Oman, see page 141).

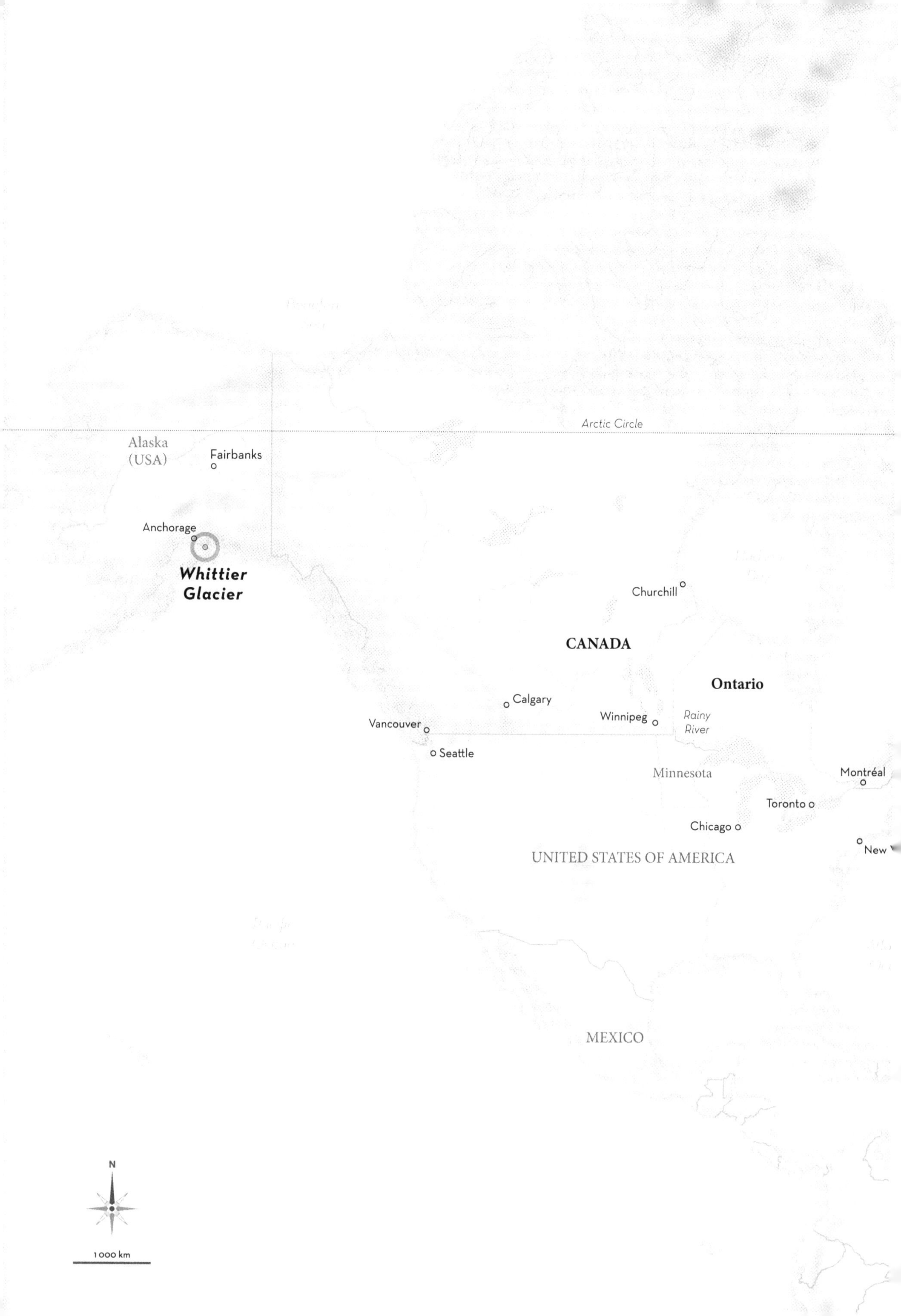

Arctic Circle

Alaska
(USA)

Fairbanks
o

Anchorage
o
o

*Whittier
Glacier*

Churchill
o

CANADA

Ontario

o Calgary

Winnipeg o

*Rainy
River*

Vancouver o

o Seattle

Montréal
o

Minnesota

Toronto o

Chicago o

o New

UNITED STATES OF AMERICA

MEXICO

N

1 000 km

Whittier · Alaska, USA

The world's only municipality under one roof

The "city" (as it insists on being referred to) of Whittier on the shores of Prince William Sound in Alaska could market itself as the world's only one-house municipality, for nearly all its 205 residents live in the 14-storey Begich Tower, Alaska's tallest building.

Whittier's history is fascinating. Not long after the Japanese bombed Dutch Harbor in the Aleutian Islands during World War II, the US Army began looking for a spot to build a secret military installation. The proposed base needed to be an ice-free port and as inaccessible as possible. Whittier was perfect, thanks to 3,500-feet peaks surrounding it and covering it in cloud for much of the year. To provide access to the Seward Highway to the north, the Army blasted a supply tunnel out of solid granite, and the Anton Anderson Memorial Tunnel remains one of Alaska's great engineering marvels. Completion of the tunnel led to construction of what at the time was the largest building in Alaska, to house more than 1,000 workers.

The Army maintained Whittier until 1960, leaving behind the Begich Towers, where most of Whittier's 205 residents live today – one third fewer than in the year 2000, when the tunnel was overhauled to accommodate auto traffic along with the Alaska Railroad.

To be precise, only 204 people reside in the skyscraper: one maverick chose to escape high-rise living by settling down in an abandoned bus in the harbour.

The tower has all necessary conveniences: shops, restaurants, a laundromat, post office, museum (down the hall from the post office), beauty salon, church and even a small B&B on the top two floors with lovely views of the Sound. There used to be a small jail there too, but it had to close for lack of offenders. One floor is occupied by the 'city government', including the mayor, known as the city manager, and three key departments: administration, public safety and public works.

The initial decision to house all the residents in one building was an attempt to minimise clearing away of snow, of which there's no shortage in Whittier in winter. When the military left in 1963, the town went into hibernation, only occasionally interrupted by the Alaska Railroad trains from Anchorage bringing tourists for glacier cruises in the Sound.

The railroad had been the mini-city's only link to the outside world (if not to count a tiny airstrip, left by the military and locally known as "Whittier International Airport") until the Whittier-bound extension of the Alaska Marine Highway was completed.

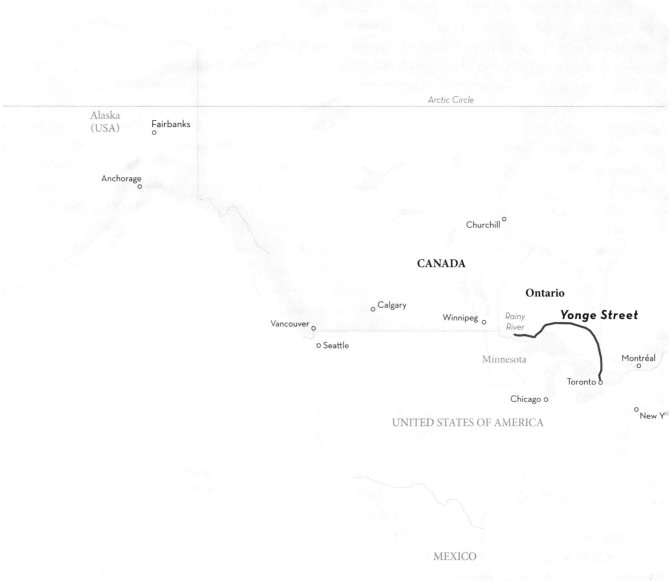

Arctic Circle

Alaska
(USA)   Fairbanks
                   o

Anchorage
        o

                                    Churchill o

                        CANADA

                                          Ontario

                        Calgary   Yonge Street
                           o
Vancouver   Winnipeg o   Rainy
        o   River
    o Seattle   Montréal
                                              o
                   Minnesota
                                    Toronto o
            Chicago o
UNITED STATES OF AMERICA
                                              o
                                               New Y

            MEXICO

   N

1 000 km

Yonge Street · Canada

The longest designated street in the world, at 1,896 km

If you ask somebody in Toronto for directions and they say "it's at the end of the street", you better make sure you're not standing on Yonge Street, where the end of the street could be 1,896 km away. Yonge Street is, in fact, the longest street in the world (according to Guinness World Records) if we stick to the Merriam-Webster Dictionary definition of 'a street' as "a thoroughfare with abutting property", not limiting it to one particular city, town or village. Even for Canadians used to huge distances, the concept of living on the same street as someone a quarter of a continent and a time zone away is a bit hard to swallow. Yonge Street roars through Toronto and straight through the Ontario wilderness into the sub-Arctic, across the top of the Great Lakes. The street ends only when it smacks straight into the US border at Rainy River, Minnesota. The trip up the street takes four days.

Yonge Street was integral to the original planning and settlement of western Upper Canada in the 1790s, forming the basis of the concession roads in Ontario today. Once the southernmost leg of Highway 11, linking the provincial capital with northern Ontario, it has been referred to as "Main Street Ontario". Today, no section of Yonge Street is marked as a provincial highway.

Ontario's first colonial administrator, John Graves Simcoe, named the street for his friend Sir George Yonge, an expert on ancient Roman roads. The first stretch, completed on 16 February 1780, was 55 km. Yonge Street – a commercial main thoroughfare rather than a ceremonial one – became important in the late eighteenth and early nineteenth centuries as one of the routes down which the furs and other riches from the north came to market in Toronto.

Rainy River on the Ontario–Minnesota border marks the spot where Yonge Street finishes. A lonely road sign reads, simply, "ENDS". Standing there, Toronto is but a distant memory.

The world's shortest street

By comparison, Ebenezer Place, in Wick, Caithness, Scotland, is credited by *Guinness World Records* as being the world's shortest street, at 2.06 metres. The street has only one address: the entrance to No. 1 Bistro, which is part of Mackays Hotel.

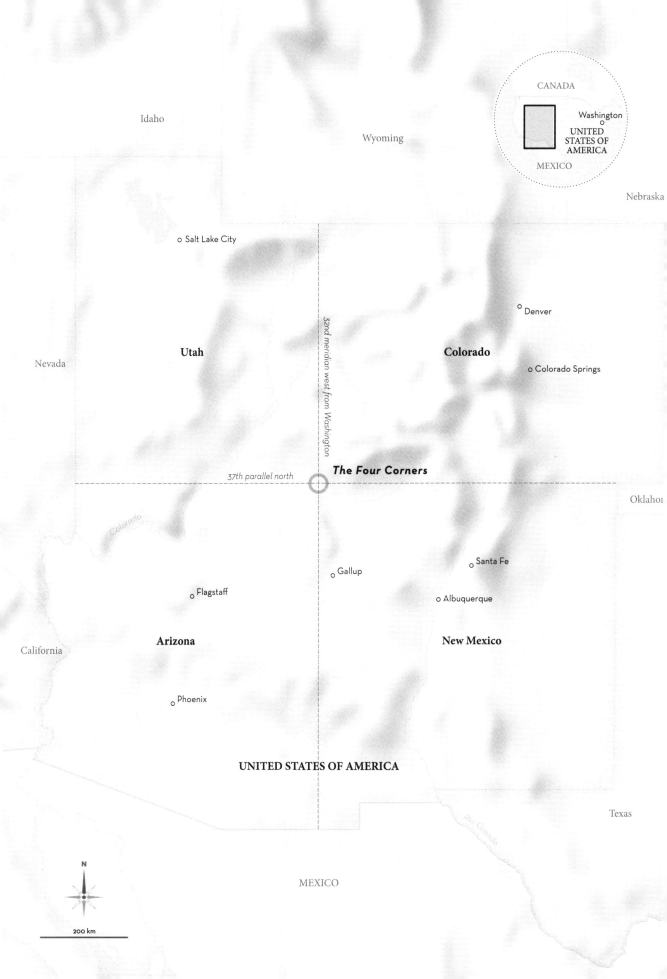

The Four Corners · USA

The only point in the USA where four states meet,
with one suing another over a border controversy

The Four Corners is a region of the south-western United States which includes the south-western corner of Colorado, the south-eastern corner of Utah, the north-eastern corner of Arizona, and the north-western corner of New Mexico. The area is named after the quadripoint where the boundaries of the four states meet.

Marked by the Four Corners Monument, the point is the only location in the United States where four states converge.

The United States acquired the region from Mexico after the end of the Mexican–American War in 1848.

The first boundary, which was defined in 1850, created the New Mexico Territory and Utah Territory. The border between the two was defined as the 37th parallel north.

In 1861, the eastern part was taken from Utah Territory to create the Colorado Territory. The Colorado Territory's southern border would remain as the 37th parallel north, but the new border between the Colorado and Utah Territories was defined as the 32nd meridian west from Washington (a reference line used at the time as the Washington meridian).

In 1863, after a claim that the New Mexico Territory was too big to be properly administered, an Arizona Territory was created by Congress, using the same borders of 37th parallel north and of the 32nd meridian west.

Since the early twentieth century, controversies have arisen regarding the accuracy of the monument's location: it was found that the borders did not always follow the lines of meridian and parallel, as intended, due to the primitive surveying technology available at the time. This discrepancy left the four states asking if the correct borders were the exact lines of meridian and parallel (and if new, more accurate, surveys needed to be done), or if the markers placed during the initial surveys were now the actual border.

For this reason, after New Mexico sued Colorado in 1919, the Supreme Court ruled in 1925 that the markers placed during the initial surveys were the actual borders, even if they were off in some locations (like in the case of the Four Corners Monument, which is roughly 550 metres east of where it should be). The issue was resolved, and today's legal description of the borders is based on the original markers, not the written description of the borders created when the territories were formed. Because of this, the borders between these states are not perfectly straight, and often zigzag.

Canada also has a four-corner area, where the provinces of Manitoba, Saskatchewan, the Northwest Territories and Nunavut meet. Nunavut was officially separated from the Northwest Territories in 1999, though the boundaries had been defined in 1993 by the Nunavut Act and the Nunavut Land Claims Agreement. Both documents define Nunavut's boundary as including the "intersection of 60°00'N latitude with 102°00'W longitude, being the intersection of the Manitoba, Northwest Territories and Saskatchewan borders".

The intersection of the boundaries of Manitoba, Saskatchewan and Northwest Territories, surveyed before the creation of Nunavut, is marked by a metre-high aluminium obelisk.

CANADA

o Winnipeg

Manitoba

Ontario

Angle
Inlet

Sprague o

*Northwest
Angle*

Roseau o

Rainy River o

International Falls o

North
Dakota

Minnesota

Grand Forks o

UNITED STATES OF AMERICA

Bemidji o

o Grand Rapids

N

100 km

Northwest Angle · USA

Reachable from the US only by boat or through Canada,
the only place outside Alaska where the US extends north of the 49th parallel
is the result of historical bad mapping

Roughly in the middle of the USA–Canada border, which at 8,900 km is the longest international frontier in the world, the borderline bends north to the Northwest Angle, the only place outside Alaska where the US extends north of the 49th parallel.

Sticking up like a chimney on the roof of Minnesota, reaching into Ontario and Manitoba in Canada, the Northwest Angle is therefore the northernmost point in the continental US. Like Point Roberts (see page 17) and Alaska, it is reachable from the US only by boat or through Canada.

This geographic oddity is a result of bad mapping in the eighteenth century and a lengthy negotiation between the US and Great Britain.

During the drafting of the Treaty of Paris (the official end to the American Revolutionary War in 1783), negotiators, including Benjamin Franklin, Minister Plenipotentiary for the USA, worked out a border from the Atlantic Ocean to the Mississippi River. After cutting across the Great Lakes, the frontier was to follow smaller lakes and rivers (such as the Rainy) from Lake Superior to Lake of the Woods. The border was then supposed to extend at a north-west angle across Lake of the Woods and cut due west to the Mississippi River.

But surveys of the area were rudimentary and negotiators in Paris were using the faulty Mitchell Map, which showed the Mississippi mistakenly extending too far north beyond its actual source at Lake Itasca. Also, the mapped shape (like a large egg) and location of Lake of the Woods were wrong. It quickly became clear the proposed borderline could not be drawn.

The error became clearer after the Louisiana Purchase (1803), which also came with unspecified borders that required mapping and negotiation.

Therefore, after the 49th parallel had been agreed as the line dividing American and British possessions west of Lake of the Woods, in 1818 another line was drawn due south from that northwesternmost point towards the 49th parallel. It created the 90-degree upward bend locals called 'The Angle'.

Several times in the nineteenth century, the British tried to negotiate, bringing the Angle back into Canada, but for historical reasons and pride, the US never wanted to change anything negotiated in the Treaty of Paris.

The Northwest Angle today spans 1,500 sq km, 1,200 of which are water. Roughly 120 US citizens are spread out along the shores of Lake of the Woods and its islands. The town has no traffic lights, hospitals or grocery stores. It does have a one-room schoolhouse, the last of its kind in Minnesota.

Citizens who want to go shopping must make a 120 km overland trek through Canada and back into Minnesota, crossing the international border twice and using gravel and dirt roads much of the way. There are no ferries across Lake of the Woods and the Northwest Angle has no direct, all-season road access to the US.

o Squamish

CANADA

Vancouver o

Nanaimo o

o Surrey

o Langley City

*Boundary
Bay*

Point Roberts

*Vancouver
Island*

o Bellingham

Langford
o   o
Victoria

UNITED STATES OF AMERICA
(Washington State)

o
Port Angeles

o Everett

o Seattle

N

o Tacoma

o Olympia

100 km

Point Roberts · USA/Canada

A peninsula in the USA that connects
by land only with Canada

Point Roberts in northern Washington state (population 1,300) is situated on a peninsula that connects by land only with Canada. For an American to reach it by land, they must cross the border twice. Territorially, therefore, it is an exclave, and the only way to get there by car from the USA is through Canada.

Under different circumstances, the isolated 1,200-hectare peninsula would have been an overlooked corner of the sprawl surrounding Greater Vancouver. But the community owes its strange existence to the 1846 Oregon Treaty, which divided the Pacific Northwest along the 49th parallel – unwittingly sealing off a small enclave of US land.

British colonial authorities offered a more accessible plot of territory in exchange, but their entreaties were stubbornly ignored and, only 40 years on, some settlers over the border laid the foundations for Canada's third largest city: Vancouver. Today, Point Roberts relies heavily on offering a miniature US to its 2.5 million next-door neighbours.

The community's five gas stations abound with British Columbia Canadian licence plates filling up with fuel at 10¢ to 30¢ less per litre than in Canada. A liquor store sells cut-rate spirits and obscure US beers and retailers offer low-price dairy products. Restaurants serve medium-rare burgers – a delicacy so scorned by British Columbia's health codes that they are virtually non-existent in Greater Vancouver.

Of the more than 2,000 houses on the peninsula, roughly 1,300 are seasonal homes for vacationing Canadians. During the summer, the population balloons to 5,000.

Many of the community's permanent residents are Canadians with green cards or joint citizenship. Vehicles fly Canucks flags and Point Roberts youngsters play in Canadian sports leagues.

Confusingly, all Point Roberts veterinarians, healthcare providers and even high schools are in mainland Washington, accessible only by two border crossings through Canadian territory, which automatically creates a kind of 'gated community'. That is not to say it is free of crime. In 2009, Ryan Alexander, the accused murderer of California model Jasmine Fiore, used the porous Point Roberts border to slip into Canada. Later, Colton Harris-Moore, the teenage "Barefoot Bandit", made a foray into Point Roberts during his two-year spree of West Coast burglaries and vehicle thefts.

Ernst Thälmann Island · Cuba

Former East Germany's sole overseas possession
and an unsolved diplomatic issue …

In 1972, when Cuban dictator Fidel Castro was on a state visit to East Berlin, he presented his GDR comrades with a gift: the small, skinny island of Cayo Blanco del Sur, located a couple miles off the coast of Cuba, about 15 km long and home to a coral reef, iguanas, endangered species, but no people.

Castro renamed the island Ernst Thälmann Island (Cayo Ernesto Thaelman in Spanish) after the doomed Weimar-era leader of the German Communist Party who was arrested in 1933 and executed at Buchenwald on Adolf Hitler's orders in 1944. Thälmann was lionised by post-war communists as an anti-fascist martyr and had many streets and schools named in his honour throughout East Germany and in the USSR.

Later in 1972, in a ceremony on the southern shores of the island, the East German ambassador to Cuba unveiled a stone bust of Thälmann before a mix of East German and Cuban comrades. The beach they stood on was christened "German Democratic Republic Beach" (Playa República Democrática Alemana).

Ernst Thälmann Island was East Germany's sole overseas possession, and was kind of a big deal for a while. In 1975, Frank Schöbel, arguably East Germany's biggest pop star, travelled to Cuba to film a music video for his song 'Insel im Golf von Cazones' ('Island in the Gulf of Cazones'). The video featured the commemorative bust of Thälmann, and footage later showed up in a documentary celebrating the great friendship between Cuba and East Germany.

In the early nineties, the Berlin Wall was torn down and reunification paperwork was drafted in Germany. A treaty on the economic, monetary and social union came into effect on 3 October 1990, but none of the documents said a word about Ernst Thälmann Island. It appeared to have been forgotten and neglected, thousands of miles away in the Caribbean.

Germany remained silent on the subject of Ernst Thälmann Island until 2001, when Thema 1, a German online newspaper and think tank, ran a report arguing it belonged to modern Germany. The whole island had been trashed by Hurricane Mitch three years earlier, with the bust of Thälmann knocked over and broken.

Cuba, still under communist rule, reacted negatively to the article and denied journalists access to the island, claiming their gift to East Germany had only been symbolic. The German Foreign Ministry concurred, telling the news service EFE that the 1972 agreement between the countries was "not a gift, but a change of name". Since then, neither country has seemed willing to press the issue.

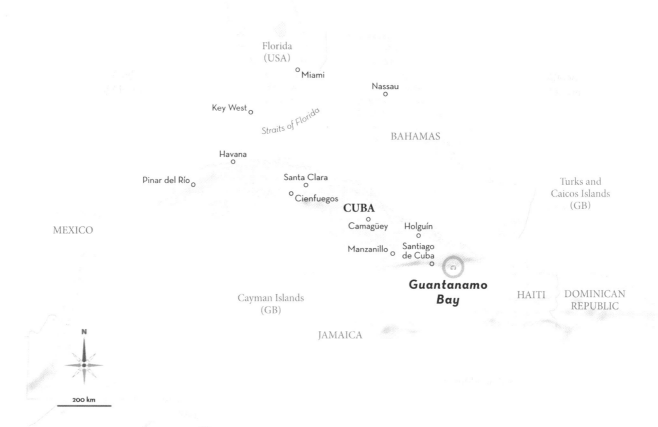

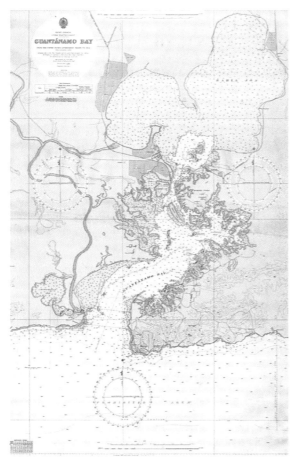

Guantanamo Bay · Cuba

A US-controlled enclave in Cuba dating back to 1903

Located in Guantanamo Province at the south-east end of Cuba, Guantanamo Bay (Spanish: Bahía de Guantánamo; population 10,000, out of whom 4,000 are US military personnel) is a famous US-controlled enclave surrounded by steep hills, which create a natural exclave cut off from its immediate hinterland. It is the largest harbour on the south side of the island.

The story of Guantanamo goes back to the four-month Spanish-American War in 1898. Ever since, it has been a source of controversy.

Until 1898, Cuba had belonged to Spain, and as the Spanish empire diminished, Cubans fought for their independence. The US joined in to help its neighbour and, though the Spanish-American War eventually focused mainly on the Spanish presence in the Philippines, Cuba was the site of the sinking of the USS *Maine*, prompting American military involvement.

When the war ended, Spain gave the US control of Cuba, among other territories, like Puerto Rico. About three years later, Cuba became an independent nation. That independence, however, was not without a catch: as part of the Platt Amendment (the document that governed the end of the occupation), the new Cuban government had to lease or sell territories to the United States. A treaty signed in 1903 and reaffirmed in 1934 meant the US recognised Cuba's "ultimate sovereignty" over the enclave of 117 sq km in Oriente province near the island's south-east end, i.e. Guantanamo Bay. In return, Cuba yielded the US "complete jurisdiction and control" through a perpetual lease that can be voided only by mutual agreement. When Fidel Castro came to power in the 1950s, there was briefly a period during which the fate of Guantanamo seemed in question. Castro threatened to kick the navy out if the US continued to interfere with the Cuban economy. In 1964, he cut off the water supply to the enclave, to which the US navy responded by building its own water and power plants.

Guantanamo returned to the news in the 1990s when it got a new set of residents: in 1991, after a coup in Haiti, thousands of Haitians fled by sea for the United States. In December of that year, Guantanamo Bay became the site of a refugee camp built to house those who sought asylum while the Bush administration figured out what to do with them.

In the years that followed, the camp became home to thousands of native Cubans, who had also attempted to flee to the US for political asylum. In 1999, during conflict in the Balkans (and after the Haitian and Cuban refugees had been sent home or to the States), the US agreed to put up 20,000 Balkan refugees at Guantanamo, before the plan was scrapped.

The decision to house al-Qaeda detainees at Guantanamo was reached shortly after 9/11. In January 2002, the US took 20 Afghan men, alleged to be members of the Taliban or al-Qaeda, to its naval base at Guantanamo. Images of the men shackled on their knees wearing orange jumpsuits in outdoor cells with concrete floors at Camp X-Ray quickly spread around the globe.

In the years that followed, hundreds more came and went. In 2021, almost two decades after the prison opened, 40 men remained there, at a cost of more than $10 million per detainee per year.

BRAZIL

PARAGUAY

CHILE URUGUAY

ARGENTINA

URUGUAY

Timoteo Dominguez Island
(Isla Timoteo Domínguez)

Martin Garcia Island
(Isla Martín García)

ARGENTINA

N

50 km

Martín Garcia Island · Argentina/Uruguay

The new and only land border between Argentina and Uruguay

Isla Martín García, or Martin Garcia Island (1.84 sq km, population 150), was until recently an Argentine enclave island off the Río de la Plata (River Plate) coast of Uruguay – fully within the boundaries of Uruguayan waters. In 1973, both countries reached an agreement declaring Martin Garcia an Argentine territory and an international nature reserve.

The strategically located island was fortified in the 1820s by Argentine forces to deny the Brazilian navy access to the Uruguay River. That fortress, named Constitucion, succeeded in keeping Brazilian reinforcements at bay during the Battle of Juncal between 8 and 9 February 1827, allowing the Argentines to destroy the Brazilian squadron on the Uruguay River during the Argentina-Brazil War.

Several Argentine political figures were kept under arrest on the island by different military governments, including presidents Hipólito Yrigoyen (1930), Juan Perón (1945) and Arturo Frondizi (1962).

Since the start of the current millennium, another sedimentary island, Timoteo Domínguez, began to emerge to the north, finally joining the original Martin Garcia island that had been growing underwater for decades as the sediments brought along by the mighty Parana and Uruguay rivers accumulated in the River Plate.

In practical terms, this means that the mid-River Plate islands have joined together, forming the only existing land (or "dry") border, despite being partially underwater, between Argentina and Uruguay, until then officially separated by the River Uruguay and the River Plate.

© Silvinarossello - Own work, Wikimedia Commons

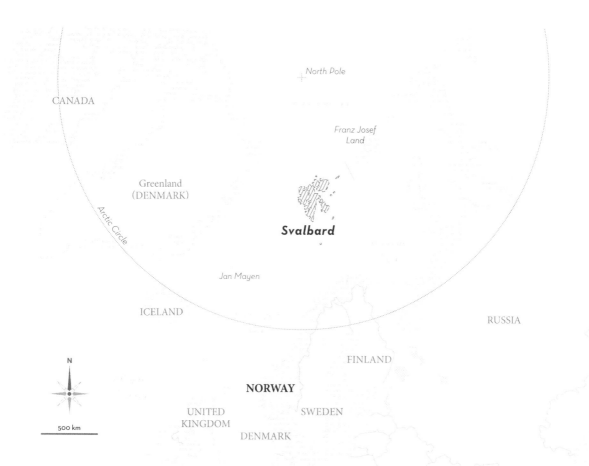

North Pole

CANADA

Franz Josef
Land

Greenland
(DENMARK)

Arctic Circle

Svalbard

Jan Mayen

ICELAND

RUSSIA

N

FINLAND

500 km

NORWAY

UNITED
KINGDOM

SWEDEN

DENMARK

Svalbard · Norway

A Norwegian territory where any country can freely exploit the local resources

A Norwegian archipelago in the Arctic Ocean, between Greenland to the west, the archipelago Franz Joseph Land to the east and Continental Europe to the south, Svalbard offers the unique authorisation for any country to freely exploit its local resources.

The origin of this status dates back to the Treaty of Spitsbergen (9 February 1920), which recognised the sovereignty of Norway over the territory in exchange for a clause stipulating it be declared a "demilitarised zone", authorising the citizens of diverse countries to exploit its natural resources "on an absolutely equal footing". Being a region abundant in coal, it was the stage for territorial disputes between Great Britain, Denmark, the Netherlands and Norway.

Today, for geopolitical reasons of presence, only Russia uses this right by continuing the extraction of coal, even if it is at a loss. After exploiting a similar establishment for many years in Pyramiden (abandoned in 2000), Russia now has only one permanent establishment, in Barentsburg.

Until the 1990s, the Russian population of Spitsbergen was greater than the Norwegian population, but it is no longer the case. Now, out of 2,500 inhabitants, the majority are Norwegian, despite the presence of about 800 Russian and Ukrainian citizens and around 15 Polish scientists.

After obtaining the full administration of the archipelago as early as 1925, Norway decided to rename it Svalbard (literally 'cold coast' in Icelandic), and kept the name of Spitsbergen ('pointed mountain') for the main island of the archipelago, which had previously been called Western Spitsbergen. It was the northernmost land of Norway, 500 km north of the continental coasts of Norway.

Its unique status has other practical consequences: it is not subject to Norwegian taxation, its surface area is not included in Norway's surface area and it is neither a member of the Schengen Area nor of the European Free Trade Association (EFTA). Foreigners are equally accepted without a tourist visa or work permit.

Although certain sources mention a discovery of the archipelago by the Icelanders or the Russians in the thirteenth century, the first uncontested discovery of the archipelago was made by Dutch navigator Willem Barents in 1596. He gave his name to the Barents Sea, between Norway, Svalbard and the island of Novaya Zemblya (Russia).

The islands were used as an international base for whaling during the seventeenth and eighteenth centuries and as a base camp for many Arctic expeditions.

Svalbard was the scene of a little-known struggle between the Third Reich and the Allies. Led by Norway from Scotland in 1942, Operation Fritham aimed to prevent the Germans installing air force bases in the archipelago and gaining possession of the island's rich coal mines.

Since February 2008, the territory has been the home of the Global Seed Vault in Svalbard, a bank of seeds belonging to the Norwegian government and funded by the Rockefeller Foundation, the Syngenta Foundation and other private organisations. It conserves (at -18°C) the seeds of trees and all food crops on the planet. At the beginning of 2017, 930,000 varieties, essentially of agricultural origin, were present in the bunker 120 metres under the ground.

Märket Island

FINLAND

Åland

Helsinki

Stockholm

Tallinn

SWEDEN

ESTONIA

RUSSIA

Gotland

Riga

LATVIA

LITHUANIA

KALININGRAD
(RUSSIA)

Vilnius

Gdansk

BELARUS

POLAND

Warsaw

UKRAINE

N

500 km

Märket island · Sweden/Finland

A small island divided between Finland and Sweden

Märket is a 3.3-hectare lump of rock, or "skerry", in the passage joining the Gulf of Bothnia to the Baltic Sea, between Sweden and Finland. The unpopulated island has been divided between the two countries since the Treaty of Fredrikshamn of 1809 defined the border between Sweden and the Russian Empire, which ruled Finland at the time. When the border was drawn by the treaty's signatories, by sheer coincidence it ran straight through Märket.

The island lies in the middle of the 11-km-wide, 27-km-long Understen–Märket passage, and was probably a useful navigation mark, which is why it was named Märket ("the mark") in Swedish.

To get more out of the island as a navigational aid, the Russians built a lighthouse there in 1885. Accidentally, the structure was erected not on the Finnish, but on the Swedish side of the island. The de facto border violation continued after Finland's independence in 1917 and was only resolved in 1981. The solution was ingenious: rather than transfer sovereignty over the lighthouse to Sweden, or physically move it to the Finnish side, the island's border itself was redrawn.

Two conditions needed to be met: the sea border was not to change, to safeguard existing fishing rights, and each country should retain a similar-sized share of the territory. The result was a complicated land swap, leaving the formerly straight border Z-shaped. The lighthouse is now on the Finnish side, in a new bit of Finland west of the former border. Next to it is a companion chunk of Sweden, east of the original border line.

Strangely, no border markers mark the border on Märket, but 10 holes were drilled into the rock to indicate its twists and turns. That is because anything less sturdy and permanent would soon be eaten up by the frequent storms and inclement winter weather. The weather and sea are so powerful that the island's very shape is subject to constant change. Every 25 years, a bi-national commission surveys the island and implements any border changes needed.

Imatra

Joutseno

Svetogorsk

Lappeenranta

Saimaa Canal

Lake Nuijamaa

FINLAND

RUSSIA

Vyborg

Maly Vysotsky Island
(Ravansaari)

Vysotsk

N

20 km

SWEDEN

FINLAND

ESTONIA

RUSSIA

LATVIA

Saimaa Canal · Russia/Finland

A canal leased by Russia to Finland, running through Russian territory

The Saimaa Canal connects Lake Saimaa (Finland) with the Gulf of Finland, near the city of Vyborg (Russia). The canal is 43 km long and connects a system of inland waterways and canals in the 120 interconnected lakes in south-central and south-east Finland (Finnish Lakeland). Nearly half the canal (19.6 km) runs through land leased from Russia to Finland. That area is not, however, part of the EU.

The unique situation of a canal leased on a long-term basis by a country to another country dates back to when it was built, between 1845 and 1856. Then it linked Lappeenranta and Viipuri (today's Vyborg in Russia), which were both part of the autonomous duchy of Finland.

In the Moscow Peace Treaty of 1940, Finland ceded the Karelian Isthmus and Vyborg to the Soviet Union. Control of the canal was divided and traffic ended.

To ensure continued use of this important communication channel, in 1963 Finland obtained a 50-year lease on the Soviet part of the canal and Maly Vysotsky Island. Finland constructed a deeper, 43-km canal, which opened in 1968.

In 2008, Russia raised the annual rent from €290,000 to €1.22 million, with revisions every 10 years.

In 2010, Finland obtained a second 50-year lease from Russia, starting in 2013, with Maly Vysotsky Island not included.

Under the latest treaty signed by the Finnish and Russian governments, Russian law is in force in the area, with a few exceptions for maritime rules and the employment of canal staff, which fall under Finnish jurisdiction. There are also special rules for foreign vessels travelling to Finland via the canal. Passports are required at the international boundaries, but Russian visas are not needed for just passing through the canal. A passport, however, must be shown and checked at the border. Euros are accepted for the canal fees throughout.

FINLAND

ESTONIA
RUSSIA

LATVIA

LITHUANIA

BELARUS

Värska Parish

RUSSIA

Verhulitsa

Lutepää

Saatse Boot

Sesniki

ESTONIA

N

RUSSIA

5 km

The Saatse Boot · Russia/Estonia

How to visit Russia without a visa

In south-east Estonia, in the municipality of Värska Parish, lies a peculiar border irregularity: a small piece of Russian land, the "Saatse Boot", juts into Estonian territory as the Russian-Estonian border twists and turns through the lake and forest landscape.

This piece of foreign land lies directly between two small Estonian villages – Lutepää and Sesniki. Traditionally, the only way to reach Sesniki from Lutepää, and vice versa, is to go through the Saatse Boot by crossing the international border twice.

When the Russia-Estonia border was drawn in 1945, Estonia was part of the Soviet Union, so crossing borders was not a big issue. But when the Soviet Union dissolved in 1991 and Estonia then joined the EU, the Saatse Boot became a thorn in Estonia's side.

Fortunately, both countries have so far been able to resolve the issue amicably. According to the agreed terms, Estonians can use the road through the Saatse Boot without the need for a Russian visa, provided they do not travel on foot. The road can only be driven (riding on a donkey is allowed too), without stopping, even to take a quick photo of this territorial oddity.

Yet, despite (or maybe because of) not being allowed to do so, many tourists dare to pose for photos in front of the very signs disallowing such activities – which can easily lead to being detained at the nearest Russian border post and forced to pay hefty fines.

If a car breaks down inside the Boot, Russian border guards will conduct an inspection. If they are satisfied the breakdown is genuine, they will authorise the Estonian border guards to tow it back to Estonia.

Lutepää and Sesniki are about 1,200 metres apart. The section of road connecting them through the Saatse Boot is about 900 metres long. That was the only way of getting to either village until 2008, when a new road opened, making it possible to reach them without passing through the Saatse Boot. But that other road, leading to Russia, involves a 15–20 km detour, so villagers and visitors still use the old one.

In 2005, Russia agreed to straighten out the border and transfer the "Boot" area to Estonia in exchange for some patches of Estonian land. That would have put an end to this geographic oddity, but the new treaty is yet to be ratified. Until that happens, the Saatse Boot will continue to attract tourists for the unique opportunity it provides to visit Russian territory without a visa.

BELARUS

Unecha

Klintsy

RUSSIA

Sankovo-
Medvezhye

Novozybkov

Homyel

UKRAINE

Chernihiv

Chernobyl

N

50 km

ESTONIA
LATVIA
LITH.
BELARUS   RUSSIA

UKRAINE
MOLDOVA

Sankovo-Medvezhye · Russia/Belarus

Russia's only existing exclave

Sankovo-Medvezhye (4.5 sq km) is part of the Zlynkovsky District of Bryansk Oblast, just 800 metres from the Russian border in an unsettled Russian exclave in Belarus.

The name of the exclave comes from the villages of Sankovo and Medvezhye which existed during Soviet times.

The origins of the two settlements can hardly be established today, with different versions referring to different events, but all amounting to a few Russian people buying this piece of land to settle.

After World War II, the settlements were cut off from the rest of Russian territory, as a strip of land connecting them to the motherland was officially transferred to the Belarus Soviet Republic. The change had no real impact on the lives of the locals, as Russia and Belarus were both parts of the USSR.

It was a very compact settlement, with a collective farm, club, store and a cemetery. Every resident had one of the four family names common in the area: Dobrodei, Pesenko, Molchanov or Spravtsev.

Soon, however, the tight community was forced to resettle. When the Chernobyl disaster happened in 1986, the post-explosion fallout affected large territories of Ukraine, Russia and Belarus. Located close to the border of these three states, the villages of Sankovo and Medvezhye had to be evacuated.

As the two villages were abandoned, the houses became dilapidated. Today, nobody lives in the area, as it is still considered to be polluted and dangerous.

It is possible to visit the exclave, with permission from the Belarus authorities, indicating a reason for the visit, as the Russian piece of land is surrounded by contaminated Belarusian forest with no way around it.

FINLAND

Åland

Helsinki

Stockholm

Tallinn

SWEDEN

ESTONIA

RUSSIA

Gotland

Riga

LATVIA

LITHUANIA

Kaliningrad
(RUSSIA)

Vilnius

Gdansk

BELARUS

POLAND

Warsaw

N

UKRAINE

500 km

Kaliningrad region · Russia

A unique territorial, administrative and historical entity

According to the definition of enclaves/exclaves (see page 7) by Dr Honore Marc Catudal from his monograph *The Exclave Problem of Western Europe* (University of Alabama Press, 1979): "An exclave is a part of one state completely surrounded by the territory of another. It cannot be situated on an international river or sea coast, share a frontier with another exclave, or border two or more countries ... Finally, an exclave may never be totally self-governing, but somehow subordinate to the home state or motherland."

Using this definition, the Kaliningrad region (population just under 1 million) – a wedge-shaped piece of land along the Baltic Sea between Poland and Lithuania with 145 km of Baltic Sea coastline – despite being frequently referred to as Russia's exclave, is a detached piece of Russian territory separated from Russia by parts of Lithuania and Belarus.

Enclave/exclave or not, Kaliningrad constitutes a unique territorial, administrative and historical entity.

Known as Konigsberg prior to its Soviet annexation from Germany after World War II, the city was founded in 1255 near the mouth of the Pregolya River. The philosopher Immanuel Kant was born in Konigsberg in 1724.

The capital of German East Prussia, Konigsberg was the home to a grand Prussian royal castle, destroyed along with much of the city in World War II.

Konigsberg was renamed Kaliningrad in 1946 after Mikhail Kalinin, the token (as opposed to Stalin) "leader" of the Soviet Union from 1919 until 1946. At the time, Germans living in the oblast were forced out, to be replaced with Soviet citizens. While there were early proposals to change the name of Kaliningrad back to Konigsberg, none succeeded.

The ice-free port of Kaliningrad on the Baltic Sea became home to the Soviet Baltic Fleet. During the Cold War, 200,000 to 500,000 soldiers were stationed in the region. Today, only 25,000 soldiers occupy Kaliningrad, an indicator of the reduction of the perceived threat from NATO countries.

In the 1970s, the USSR attempted to build in Kaliningrad a 22-storey House of Soviets, one of the ugliest buildings on Russian soil, but the structure was erected on terrain with many underground tunnels and began to slowly collapse. It still stands there, unoccupied.

After the fall of the USSR, neighbouring Lithuania and former Soviet republics gained their independence, cutting Kaliningrad off from Russia. Kaliningrad was supposed to develop in the post-Soviet era into a Porto Franco and "Hong Kong of the Baltic", but all-permeating corruption keeps most investment away.

South Korean-based Kia Motors has a car factory in Kaliningrad, where some pre-World War II Konigsberg structures still stand, including the famous zoo, train station, a couple of bridges and a handful of impressive suburban cottages.

The remaining pre-World War II German-built roads and motorways are still hugely superior to the newly-laid Soviet and Russian ones.

The town of Baltiysk (German name Pillau), just outside Kaliningrad, formerly a "secret" Soviet town closed to all foreigners, is the only Russian Baltic Sea port said to be ice-free all year round, so plays an important role in the maintenance of the Baltic Fleet, most of which is based there.

o Vinnytsya

UKRAINE

o Suceava

o Balti

o Rybnitsa

Transnistria

MOLDOVA

o Dubasari

Chisinau o

Benderi o   o Tiraspol

o Mykolayiv

o Odessa

ROMANIA

Galati o   o Reni

Tulcea

N

o Constanta

BULGARIA

100 km

Transnistria

The country that does not exist

Situated within the official territory of Moldova, in the eastern part of the former Soviet republic of Moldavia and at the border with Ukraine, the self-proclaimed Transnistria Republic (population 470,000) has been a de facto independent state since the end of the USSR in 1991. Although it is not recognised by the UN, it has a border, an army, a currency, produces stamps, etc.

Historically, it was first under the control of the Kievan Rus (until the end of the thirteenth century) and then the Polish–Lithuanian Commonwealth (1569–1795). As a result of numerous wars and annexations, by the beginning of the nineteenth century the Russian Empire incorporated both Bessarabia – a historical region bounded by the Dniester river on the east and the Prut river on the west – and Transnistria, although under different administrations. Following the Russian Revolution of 1917, Bessarabia became a 'Moldavian Democratic Republic' (MDR). An autonomous entity within the proposed Russian Federation, it declared independence and united with Romania in 1918.

The Romanian rule over Bessarabia was, however, not recognised by the newly founded (1921) USSR, which considered Transnistria to be a part of the Soviet Union.

In 1940, the USSR annexed Bessarabia, the southern part of which was transferred to the Ukrainian SSR. The rest became a 'Moldavian Soviet Socialist Republic' (MSSR) within the Soviet Union.

The Moldavian SSR was formed from a part of Bessarabia (taken from Romania on June 28, following the Molotov–Ribbentrop Pact), where the majority of the population were Romanian speakers, and a strip of land on the left bank of the Dniester in the Ukrainian SSR, which was transferred to it in 1940 and was roughly equivalent to the territory of today's Transnistria.

In 1941, after Axis forces invaded Bessarabia, Romania gained control of the entire region between the Dniester and the Southern Bug rivers, including the Ukrainian city of Odessa. The territory, called the Governorate of Transnistria, was divided into 13 counties.

The Soviet Union regained the area in spring 1944, when the Soviet Army advanced into the territory, driving out the Axis forces.

After the war, the divide – created by the disproportionate settlement of Russian speakers in Transnistria compared with Bessarabia (up to 300,000 settled in MSSR in the period 1944–59) – developed further and became an increasing source of tension during the 1980s.

Following the collapse of the USSR (1991), Transnistria found itself populated mostly by ethnic Russians and Ukrainians, who refused to be incorporated into the new, independent Moldova, which had Romanian as its official national language (the Moldovan language being officially regarded as a dialect of Romanian). A military conflict with Moldova followed.

The warring sides were eventually separated in 1992 by the intervention of the 14th Russian Army under the command of General Alexander Lebed – a popular and charismatic Soviet leader. The Russian army's operational group, numbering 1,500 soldiers, is still stationed in Transnistria.

The area, which used to be famous for its fine wine, incorporates two cities (Tiraspol and Benderi) and numerous villages and towns where monuments to Lenin still adorn the streets. Almost everything – including a fair amount of illicit arms trade – is under the strict control of the state and the Soviet-style KGB (secret police).

Life in the republic is dire, yet military hysteria is constantly being whipped up, and youngsters face compulsory recruitment to the local, Cossack-style 'army' preparing for a final showdown with Moldova.

Many of Transnistria's estimated 20,000 annual visitors come on day trips from Moldova. Indeed, with regular buses from Chisinau to Tiraspol and visa-free entry to Transnistria (a hotel reservation must be produced at the border posts maintained by the Transnistrian military to stay more than one day), it is relatively easy to visit.

On 15 November 2020, voters in Moldova ousted their pro-Russian president, Igor Dodon, electing Maia Sandu, the pro-Western, Harvard-educated former prime minister, who immediately announced that she wanted the Russian peacekeeping forces out of Transnistria. The demand was not taken well by the Kremlin.

GERMANY

Hüfingen

Engen

Blumberg

Tengen

Singen (Hohentweil)

Büttenhardt

Thayngen

Herblingen

Büsingen

Schaffhausen

Ramsen

Neuhausen

***Büsingen
am Hochrhein***

Frauenfeld

SWITZERLAND

Winterhur

FRANCE   GERMANY

SWITZERLAND   AUSTRIA

ITALY

N

10 km

Zürich

Büsingen am Hochrhein · Germany/Switzerland

An enclave where you can order the drinks in Germany and consume them in Switzerland – but residents probably can't afford to …

Büsingen am Hochrhein (or simply Büsingen), population 1,450, is hard to find on maps. The small German enclave in Switzerland is a suburb of the Swiss town of Schaffhausen, where the residents of Büsingen routinely shop. The normally erratic Swiss-German border goes haywire in the Büsingen-Schaffhausen area. It even runs across the beer garden of a Büsingen pub with tables in Switzerland and the bar in Germany.

The reason for this frontier madness is that, economically, Büsingen is Swiss, but politically it is German. It is not part of the EU, instead having a customs union with Switzerland. Büsingen is excluded from the EU VAT area, so Swiss VAT generally applies. As a result Büsingers, who are paid in Swiss francs but remain predominantly German citizens, have to pay high German income taxes. Most locals agree, it is terrible.

True, Swiss prices are also high, but the taxes are relatively low. In Germany it is the other way around: lower prices and huge taxes. In Büsingen, therefore, they have the worst of both worlds.

Of course, Büsingers are free to shop in Switzerland, but those willing to work there (let alone live) need a hard-toobtain permit, normally granted after many years of residence.

German inventiveness and practicality help Büsingers ease the burden of their duality, if only slightly. The villagers have their own car number plates – "BUS" – but two postcodes: Swiss and German. In the village centre, next to modern Bürgerhaus, are Swisscom and Deutsche Telekom phone boxes, sparing locals the expense of international calls when phoning the nearest cinema or supermarket.

In their daily trials, the residents of modern Büsingen are reaping the consequences of their own ancestors' unforgiving pride – better known as stubbornness. In April 1693, Eberhard Im Thurn, a popular ruler of then Austrian Büsingen, was kidnapped and put in prison in Schaffhausen for a religious offence – angering villagers. He was released in 1699, but Büsingers had a long memory, and when Schaffhausen tried to incorporate the village into the Swiss federation in 1723, they refused. Eventually, Büsingen fell under German control, where it remains as a living reproach to Schaffhausen for the mistreatment of its leading citizen.

During the Napoleonic era, French, Austrian and Russian troops fought battles to control Büsingen, which frequently changed hands. French troops were quartered in the village for a while and the Russian Tsar Alexander plundered it in search of provisions. After the Treaty of Pressburg in 1805, Büsingen became part of Württemberg and, five years later, was incorporated into the Grand Duchy of Baden. That was absorbed into the German Reich in 1871. Since the end of World War I, Büsingers have campaigned for incorporation into Switzerland – a movement that was suppressed by the Weimar Republic police and ignored by Hitler's government.

In an interesting episode shortly after World War II, the French occupation authorities discovered Büsingen and wanted it. Although surrounded by neutral Switzerland, it legally belonged to their zone of occupation in Germany. The Swiss, fearing a violation of their much-valued neutrality, barred access to Büsingen by the French, or any other foreign troops. After prolonged negotiations, agreement was reached and a squad of French soldiers was allowed to cross Swiss territory to occupy the village.

The German-appointed, post-war mayor of Büsingen – Herr Hugo, an engineer from Hanover – unexpectedly sided with the villagers in their pro-Swiss position. He even changed all the German village signs into Swiss ones. After two months the maverick mayor was recalled by the German authorities, but refused to leave Büsingen, and lived there as an independent citizen until his death in 1959.

o Hüfingen

GERMANY

o Engen

o Blumberg

o Tengen

 Verenahof o
Büttenhardt o

o Singen (Hohentweil)

Thayngen o

Herblingen o

Schaffhausen o

Büsingen

o Ramsen

Neuhausen o

*Bodensee
(Lake Constance)*

Rhein

SWITZERLAND

Frauenfeld
o

Winterhur
o

GERMANY

FRANCE

SWITZERLAND AUSTRIA

ITALY

N

10 km

o Zürich

Verenahof · Germany

A little-known and peaceful redrawing of Germany's border after World War II

Disenclavement is a process of absorption of an enclave or an exclave by the home or the host state. The only European enclave to lose its status in the last 70 years is Verenahof – a patch of farmland of approximately 18 acres which, until 1967, was part of the German commune Wiechs am Randen near Buttenhardt, about 450 metres from the German border, i.e. a full-scale German enclave in Switzerland.

Its origins go back to the Middle Ages, when the Verena church (or nunnery, according to another source) owned this portion of uncultivated land.

Verenahof's highly unusual status was the product of the extreme irregularity of the German–Swiss border which, unlike most 'normal' frontiers, does not seem to follow the features of the landscape, but bends and zigzags unexpectedly.

Through the ages, there were numerous futile attempts by both countries to straighten it, and during one effort the status of Verenahof became an issue.

Schaffhausen (in Switzerland) had two chances to acquire Verenahof: in 1516 and in 1522, when Count Christoph von Tengen offered to sell it at a bargain price. But, both times, the city elders refused his offers. When they changed their minds several years later, the von Tengen family no longer wanted to sell.

In the aftermath of the Napoleonic wars, when Talleyrand – one of Napoleon's most trusted lieutenants – pressurised the fragmented German states to merge into the Confederation of the Rhine, Verenahof fell under the jurisdiction of the Grand Duchy of Baden. With the creation of a united Germany in 1871, it became an outlying part of the German Reich, while completely owned by its Swiss residents (farmers), who were required by the Swiss authorities to register as "overseas Swiss" at the Swiss consulate in Freiburg (Germany). That is despite the "overseas" territory being part of the small Swiss village of Buttenhardt in the centre of the Swiss canton of Schaffhausen!

Since 1854, when Verenahof was excluded from the German Customs area and until its disenclavement in 1967, its status was not dissimilar to that of Busingen (see page 43): its only residents – three families of farmers – paid high German taxes on their Swiss franc earnings. The main difference was that, being Swiss citizens, not German, Verenahof families could not vote in German elections. And, as "overseas Swiss", they were not allowed to participate in Swiss municipal elections or be elected to local (village and/or town) councils.

Also, due to the endless red tape required for a routine German police visit to Verenahof, the minuscule German exclave ended up being de facto administered by the village authorities of Buttenhardt (hard-to-obtain permissions from the Swiss authorities had to be obtained for armed "foreign" policemen to cross Swiss territory, even if only a couple of hundred yards of it. The Swiss have always been extremely touchy about foreigners with weapons on their neutral terrain).

By November 1964 when, after eight years of painstaking negotiations, Germany and Switzerland finally signed a treaty providing for Verenahof's absorption by Switzerland (the treaty went into effect on 4 October 1967), its dwellers had come to refer to themselves as neither German nor Swiss, but as "Buttenhardters"!

It was actually not so much an absorption as a swap, which had to be agreed between Germany and Switzerland, whereby the latter donated 18 acres of territory to Germany in exchange for Verenahof. After years of deliberation, an unpopulated, infertile and rock-strewn patch directly adjoining the German border was offered. The Germans, naturally, were not happy with such an exchange, and the difference in the quality of land had to be compensated with the sum of 600,000 Swiss francs. This little-known, peaceful "annexation" signified the first and only (even if ever so slight) redrawing of Germany's border since World War II.

The 1967 disenclavement proved not just that European borders could be redrawn without military conflict, but also that age-old territorial disputes between countries could be resolved peacefully and to mutual satisfaction – an important lesson taught to the world by this tiny patch of farmland.

The story of four Nazis taking refuge in Verenahof

In April 1945, three German soldiers, led by senior SS officer Colonel von Hartlein, took refuge in Verenahof and claimed they were in Germany (which they were indeed!) and hence out of reach of the French occupational forces, stationed across the German border several hundred yards away. A mini-diplomatic crisis ensued. The Swiss authorities in Berne were tipped off, and they alerted the French, who quickly realised they had no power to extract the Germans, for to "occupy" Verenahof they had to cross the territory of neutral Switzerland. To make matters worse, the Swiss farmers of Verenahof did not mind harbouring the Germans at all, and were staunchly refusing all demands from Berne to extradite them or, at least, to stop giving them food, which clashed with their notion of hospitality. "We are farmers, and we will always feed our guests, no matter where they come from," they were reported as saying.

An agreement was reached between the French and the Swiss whereby the French would allow a small contingent of Swiss policemen to enter German Verenahof (of which the French were theoretically in control, although they couldn't set foot in it) to arrest the Nazis and frogmarch them across 450 metres of Swiss territory to the German border, where they would be handed to the French. And that is precisely what happened. The locals later reminisced that the farmers were not at all pleased with the incursion. The Nazis, naturally, were even less pleased, and the well-groomed Colonel von Hartlein was, allegedly, unhappy his Swiss police escort was of a lower rank than he was.

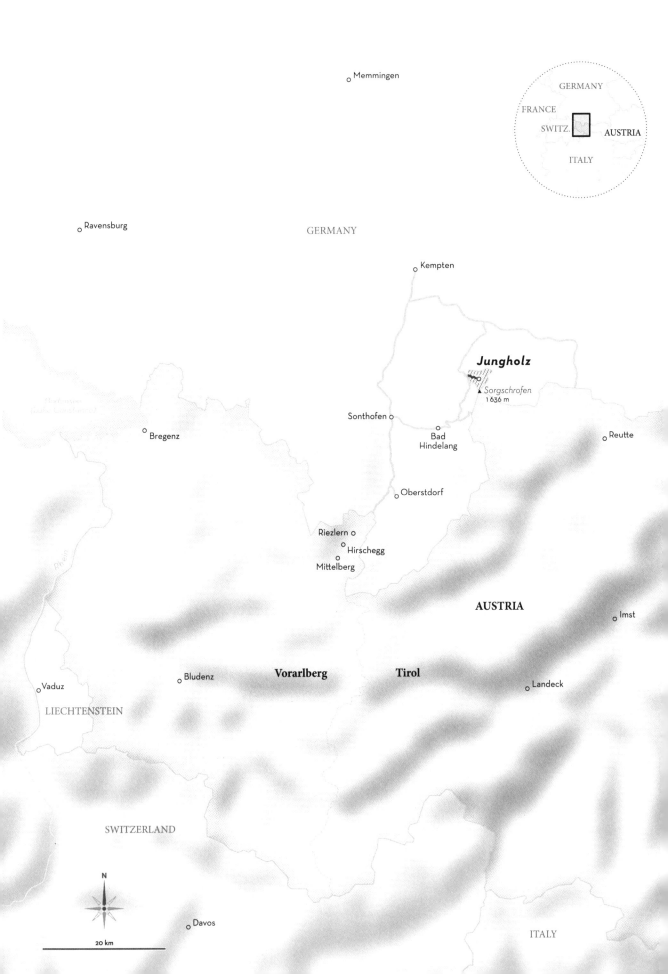

Memmingen

GERMANY

Ravensburg

Kempten

Jungholz

▲ *Sorgschrofen*
1 636 m

Sonthofen

Bad
Hindelang

Reutte

Bregenz

Oberstdorf

Riezlern
Hirschegg
Mittelberg

AUSTRIA

Imst

Vorarlberg

Tirol

Bludenz

Landeck

Vaduz

LIECHTENSTEIN

SWITZERLAND

N

Davos

ITALY

20 km

GERMANY

FRANCE

SWITZ.

AUSTRIA

ITALY

Jungholz · Austria/Germany

An Austrian village that is accessible by road only from Germany

Jungholz is an Austrian village (population 300) in the district of Reutte in the state of Tyrol, with the peculiarity of only being accessible from Germany. The only roads that connect Jungholz with the rest of the world go to Germany, not Austria, to which it belongs.

It is connected to the rest of Austria at a single point, hardly reachable, which is the summit of the mountain Sorgschrofen (1,636 metres). It is a so-called pene-enclave (or semi-enclave – see page 7), all but lost in the Bavarian Alps.

With just over 300 residents spread over 7 sq km, the village is located on a plateau, which accounts for the relatively warm, sunny climate all year round. It started from a small German farmstead, sold to a Tyrolean owner in 1342. When the first borders between Austria and Germany were drafted in 1463, the village was given to Austrian Tyrol, at which point the ongoing duality began. The Germans (Bavarians) kept trying to reclaim Jungholz peacefully until 1773, when the frontiers were finally agreed. After the Napoleonic Wars, the whole of Austrian Tyrol was incorporated into Bavaria, apart from Jungholz, which was omitted from all annexation protocols. Similar to some other European enclaves, Jungholz owes its status to a historical mistake. Unable to correct it, the Bavarian authorities chose to make Jungholz a tax-free haven, which it remains until now, if only to an extent: all German food in the village was tax-free, but alcohol wasn't.

During World War I, the men of Jungholz fought in the Austrian army, yet during World War II they had to enlist in the Wehrmacht, for the village had been temporarily reattached to Germany to become part of its Sorgschrofen district from 1938–45.

In the 1950s, the village received two phone codes – German and Austrian. Now, Jungholz can be dialled from Austria using the 056 Austrian code, but from the neighbouring German settlements using the 083 German one. Every phone number in Jungholz can be accessed by either country's code, but calling Austria from Jungholz is a local call while calls to Germany are at international rates. Postal services are regulated in a more logical way. Letters can be sent at national rates from both countries, using either of the village's two post codes – "D-87491 Jungholz (Oberallgau)" from Germany, and "A-6691 Jungholz (Tyrol)" from Austria, but letters from all other countries are supposed to use only the German code.

The village receives its water and electricity from Germany, residents vote in Austrian elections, but use the superb German National Health System. They are the world's only non-Germans entitled to use the German Health Insurance Scheme.

The nearest Austrian town of Reuter is the home of a tiny police station responsible for law and order in Jungholz. It takes weapons-carrying Austrian gendarmes about 30 minutes to reach the village via Germany – a procedure regulated by a special bilateral agreement. The same agreement stipulates that, in an emergency, German polizei are allowed to operate in Jungholz too.

The village's only primary school offers its pupils an Austrian curriculum, taught in Allemansch – High German – by German teachers.

The village is considered by some experts to be the world's wealthiest spot, with the highest rate of deposited money per household – due to being home to three big German banks. The banks operate with two SWIFT codes, Austrian and German, meaning that money can be transferred to and from Germany with no fees or taxes. But they are regulated by extremely strict Austrian banking laws, barring German auditors from accessing the records.

Memmingen

GERMANY

Ravensburg

Kempten

Sorgschrofen
1 636 m

Sonthofen

Bad
Hindelang

Bregenz

Reutte

Oberstdorf

2 036 m

1 706 m

2 230 m
Riezlern
1 702 m

2 038 m

1 982 m
Hirschegg

Kleinwalsertal valley

Mittelberg
2 321 m

2 092 m
2 533 m
2 384 m

2 131 m

AUSTRIA

Imst

Bludenz

Vorarlberg

Tirol

Landeck

Vaduz

LIECHTENSTEIN

SWITZERLAND

N

Davos

ITALY

20 km

GERMANY

FRANCE

SWITZ.
AUSTRIA

ITALY

Kleinwalsertal valley · Austria/Germany

An Austrian valley with no road connection to Austria

Kleinwalsertal valley (population 5,000) is an Austrian semi-enclave (see page 7) in Germany. Part of Austria, it has no road connection to the rest of the Vorarlberg area or with Austria, and is only accessible via Germany on a unique road in the Oberstdorf area.

Unlike Jungholz (see page 49), however, it is connected to Germany at not one, but three points, all high in the mountains and accessible only to well-trained mountaineers, in summer.

The oblong, narrow, small valley (45 sq km) has three villages: Riezlern, Hirschegg and Mittelberg.

Kleinwalsertal's dichotomy began in 1453 when the valley became Austrian. Since then, it has changed hands a number of times and was finally returned to Austria in 1945 after the 1938 annexation by Germany.

Like most of the enclaves and semi-enclaves, Kleinwalsertal has two international phone codes. It does, however, have six postcodes – two for each of its three village post offices.

Before the euro, taxes in the valley (slightly lower than in the rest of Austria) were calculated in Austrian shillings, yet payable in German marks. The same was true about Austrian postage stamps. The valley's free buses were run by a German company, and the residents were allowed to choose between Austrian or German health insurance schemes.

As part of the German economic area, Kleinwalsertal is patrolled by armed German customs officers, imposing quotas on certain Austrian goods to be "imported" into the Austrian valley. Prior to 1891, Austrian cows, wine, cheese, lard and spirits were allowed in duty-free.

In the eighteenth century, there was a peculiar regulation stating any carriage driven by a resident of Kleinwalsertal had to make way for a German vehicle when coming face to face with it on the only (and, naturally, one-lane) road connecting the valley with the nearest German town of Oberstdorf. Even now, an Austrian subject detained by Kleinwalsertal police theoretically has the right to ask for asylum in Germany, when (and if) driven to "mainland" Austria along the same road. That is why the valley's gendarmes, reportedly, prefer to transport detainees by helicopter.

After World War II, the residents of Kleinwalsertal were reluctant to grant the Germans building permissions in the valley, but soon the situation began to reverse. The power of German investment and superior technology was irresistible. One example was that phone lines from Kleinwalsertal to Germany were always perfect, whereas the ones to Austria were invariably faulty. These days, Germany dominates the valley economically.

The name of the valley derives from the Walser people (or the Walsers), one of Europe's most ancient ethnic minorities and descendants of pre-historic nomads. They came to what is now Kleinwalsertal from Bernese Oberland (Switzerland) in the thirteenth century. They soon spread over other Alpine valleys, where they set up numerous organic farms – the first of their kind in Europe. The Walsers established their own independent mini-state, with its centre in Tannberg. Their sovereignty, however, was ended in 1451 by the invasion of Sigmund, Count of Tyrol, which made Kleinwalsertal part of Austria. Organic farmers and cattle breeders, the Walsers had to move higher up the mountains (they were used to high-altitude farming), but many continue to live in the valley in resplendent, peculiar, brick and wood dwellings.

NETHERLANDS

o Maastricht

Aachen
(Aix-la-Chapelle)
o

o Raeren

Herbesthal o

Münsterbildchen

Rotgener Wald

Liège
o

Eupen o

Fringshaus
o

Rückschlag

Mützenich

o Monschau (Montjoie)

Ruitzhof
o
Kalterherberg

GERMANY

High Fens (Hautes Fagnes)

BELGIUM

Weywertz o

Malmedy o

o Bütgenbach

Trois-Ponts o

o Losheim

Vennbahn

Sankt Vith o

Auel
o

Oudler o

Troisvierges o

LUXEMBOURG

N

20 km

Vennbahn · Belgium/Germany

A former railway in Germany that belongs to Belgium

Built from 1881 to 1889 by the Prussian State to connect the industrial centre of Rothe Erde, east of Aachen (Aix-la-Chapelle), to the city of Luxembourg by the shortest route possible, the Vennbahn was a railroad mostly used to transport coal and iron. It was given to Belgium by the Treaty of Versailles (1919) in the aftermath of World War I, along with the more famous cantons of Eupen and Malmedy, as it was of particular economic importance for those two towns.

More precisely, part of Vennbahn, namely "the trackbed, with its buildings between Raeren and Kalterherbert", was to be ceded to Belgium, whereas the resulting five enclaves (between the western part of the Vennbahn and mainland Belgium – see the map) were to "remain part of Germany".

The five German enclaves (from north to south – Munsterbildchen, Rotgener Wald, Rückschlag, Mützenich and Ruitzhof) on the stretch were retained. Freight charges could be paid in German or Belgian currency, and countless strict German regulations about ticket offices, waiting rooms, noticeboards, left luggage, etc. were all accepted by the Belgians.

Both countries ran customs controls for German and Belgian passengers at both ends of the section. Conductors, pointsmen and other railway workers could be Belgian or German, but train drivers had to be exclusively Belgian nationals.

On 18 May 1940, Adolf Hitler ordered that Belgium's *cantons de l'Est* be reannexed, and Vennbahn was triumphantly returned to service as a fully German railway line. During World War II, it was in much use supplying the German army until it was all but destroyed by the Allied offensive in the winter of 1944–45. Scarcely a viaduct was spared, and it was not until 1947 that Vennbahn was partially reopened under Belgian ownership.

By 1990, the railway had become commercially unviable, and the local community tried to raise money to transform it into a tourist attraction.

That unique status has been preserved until now, despite the ending of all railway activities in 2008 due to a special bilateral agreement, according to which the former trackbed, even if no longer in use, will stay Belgian. That means the enclaves will remain intact too.

The last section of former track, between Auel and Oudler, was asphalted in 2019, and all 128 km of Vennbahn became one of Europe's longest public cycling paths. Uniquely, it retains its enclave-forming capacity.

The Vennbahn initially created seven German exclaves and one Belgian. One German exclave was finally ceded entirely to Belgium and ceased to exist. Two merged together to become one. Currently, the number of German exclaves is five. These regions are separated from mainland Germany by the trackbed of the Vennbahn, a narrow strip of land less than 20 metres across. The smallest of these exclaves, Rückschlag, is only 1.6 hectares and contains a single house with a garden. The Belgian counter-enclave is a traffic island inside a three-way German road intersection near Fringshaus.

The standard gauge line ran for about 75 km across the High Fens (Hautes Fagnes in French, Hohes Venn in German) to the south of Aachen (Aix-la-Chapelle) in a southward direction from Eupen via Raeren (the site of the depot), Monschau (Montjoie) and Malmedy to Trois-Ponts, with a 20 km eastward branch from Oberweywertz to Bütgenbach and Losheim (Hellentha). At Eupen it connected with another line to Herbesthal, where it joined the Brussels-Cologne main line. At Trois-Ponts it connected with the Liège-Luxembourg line.

By international regulations, not just the track, but five metres of land on both sides of it, with all the buildings and installations, belong to the country that owns the railway.

Breda

NETHERLANDS
GERMANY
BELGIUM
FRANCE

Gilze

Goirle

Chaam

NETHERLANDS

Alphen

Meerle

*Baarle-
Nassau*

Poppel

*Baarle-
Hertog*

Weelde

Hoogstraten

Zondereigen

Wortel

Ravels

BELGIUM

Merksplas

Rijkevorsel

Beerse

Turnhout

Arendonk

Vosselaar

N

5 km

Baarle · Belgium/Netherlands

The split-personality village south of Breda with two of everything where you might not even know what country you are in

Welcome to Baarle, probably the world's most baffling village. The only people who do not seem confused are the locals, with their proud explanation: "We are neither Belgian nor Dutch: we are Baarlenars!"

Everyone else is likely to remain confused in this village of 9,000 people on the Belgian-Dutch border where you can walk through the front door in one country and out the back in another. In a 20-minute walk you could cross the border 50 times. Three houses next to each other can have one in Belgium, one in the Netherlands and the third split between the two. The confusion is such that every building has to be marked, under the number, with a tiny Dutch or Belgian flag.

During the 2020 pandemic, a Baarle clothes shop straddling the border found itself half-open and half-closed as the two countries adopted different measures to tackle the outbreak. Belgium closed all non-essential stores to slow the spread of COVID-19, but the Dutch only required social distancing. The store's Belgian half was cordoned off, with customers in the Dutch section wanting underwear disappointed when they saw the underclothes were in Belgium.

In a theme extended to other aspects of the village, it has two names: Baarle-Nassau (Dutch) and Baarle-Hertog (Belgian). There are also two mayors, two sets of political parties, two councils, fire brigades racing each other to emergencies, post offices, two refuse collection services, and so on. It is the only village in the world where two police forces share not only the same station building, but also the same rooms, with filing cabinets painted in Dutch or Belgian colours.

The Baarle border resembles the electrocardiogram of a patient on the brink of a heart attack, thoughtlessly leaping across streets and squares, cutting through houses, offices and pubs, and even dissecting the rubbish dump. Why? It is as complex as the village itself, but Baarle is the only place in the world to have the so-called sub-enclaves (or counter-enclaves), i.e. Dutch enclaves that are within the Belgian enclaves that are within the Netherlands.

The split personality started in 1198, when the Duke of Brabant ceded most of his estate in Baarle to the Lord of Breda. Some parcels were already let out on hire and stayed the property of the Duke. Henry I, Duke of Brabant, kept these parcels to collect the land tax.

The 22 Belgian and eight Dutch enclaves making up modern Baarle are a huge improvement on 1648, when the Nassau lands were given to the northern part of the Greater Netherlands (now Holland) while the Brabant plots went to the southern part (now Belgium). With today's border being 8 km south of Baarle, the Duke of Brabant's 22 parcels of land are stranded as Belgian enclaves within the Netherlands. But there is also a Dutch enclave on the Belgian side of the border, and seven more Dutch enclaves are stranded within Belgian enclaves.

Confusing, but villagers make the most of it. Local women know that if the border runs through a house, it is better for a baby to be born on the Belgian side, because child benefits are higher there. Residents routinely buy medicines at the Belgian pharmacy, where they are less strict with prescriptions, but flowers, cheese and spirits at Dutch shops, where they are cheaper. Young drinkers refused service in the Netherlands, where the drinking age is 18, can walk across the road to Belgium, where it is 16. Baarle, perhaps more than anywhere else on the planet, offers the best of both worlds.

Claridge's Hotel · London, Great Britain

Suite 212

Declared Yugoslavian territory for one day
so that Crown Prince Alexander II could be born on his own country's soil

On 17 July 1945, the United Kingdom may have become a little smaller, and Yugoslavia a little bigger. How come? During World War II, King Peter II of Yugoslavia and his wife were exiled and spent most of the war living in Claridge's Hotel, London.

The time came for the birth of the king's son and heir to the throne. The heir had to be born on Yugoslav soil, so suite 212 of Claridge's is said to have become Yugoslav territory for a day on 17 July 1945 on the orders of Winston Churchill. There are rumours that soil from Yugoslavia was even placed under the bed where the queen gave birth. This story features on Claridge's website, which states: "At the request of Winston Churchill, suite 212 is declared Yugoslavian territory so that Crown Prince Alexander II could be born on his own country's soil."

It is also mentioned on The Royal Family of Serbia website, which reads: "On 17 July 1945 while living in Claridge's Hotel, Queen Alexandra gave birth to a son – HRH Crown Prince Alexander of Yugoslavia. Crown Prince Alexander, the heir to the throne, was born on Yugoslav territory as the British Government under the orders of Prime Minister Sir Winston Churchill declared suite 212 in Claridge's Hotel Yugoslav territory. His Holiness Patriarch Gavrilo of Serbia baptized the newborn Crown Prince in Westminster Abbey with Godparents King George VI and HRH Princess Elizabeth (now HM The Queen Elizabeth II)."

No other evidence of the temporary enclave has been found. Speaking to the BBC in 2016 about the king's deal with Winston Churchill, Crown Prince Alexander said: "Unfortunately, all the files long ago disappeared from my father's office."

Some other temporary enclaves:
- **Camp Zeist,** a former United States Air Force base in the Netherlands was, in 2000, temporarily declared sovereign territory of the United Kingdom, to allow the Pan Am Flight 103 (Lockerbie) bombing trial to take place.
- In 1943, **the maternity ward at the Ottawa Civic Hospital** in Canada was temporarily extra-territorial so that Princess Juliana's daughter, Princess Margriet, would have Dutch (through her parents' nationality) instead of dual nationality, because of her potential birth on Canadian soil. Dual nationality would have excluded her from royal succession.
- In 1979, at **Sender Zehlendorf,** East Germany, an area of 300 metres in radius around a radio tower construction site was made an exclave of the Soviet Union. A Soviet fighter plane had collided with a transmissions mast, causing it to collapse, and the Soviet Union agreed to rebuild it. Stricter German safety regulations would have slowed construction, so the area was declared a Soviet exclave for the duration of the work.

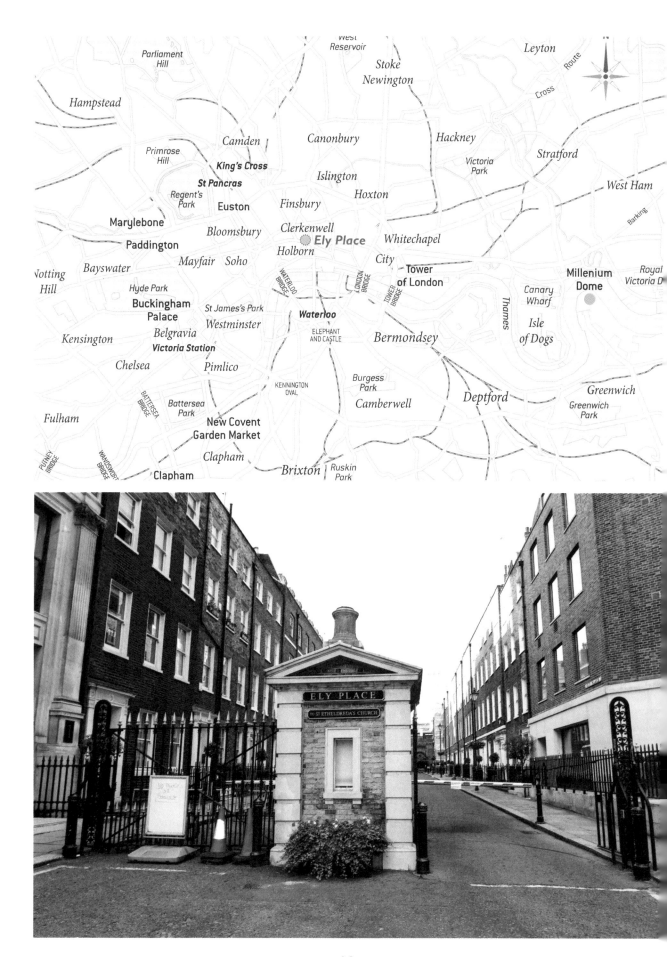

Ely Place ·
London, Great Britain

The last privately owned street in the British capital
is not geographically part of London

Ely Place is a quiet little cul-de-sac off Holborn Circus in central London, with ornate iron gates separating this street from the hustle and bustle of the city and leading to a straight, treeless lane. It is the last privately owned street in the British capital and the former residence of the Bishops of Ely, but is not geographically part of London. It is a little corner of Cambridgeshire, still enjoying freedom from entry by the London police, except by the invitation of the Commissioners of Ely Place – its own elected governing body which changes every year. The results of the latest elections, duly dated and certified by the "Clerk to the Commissioners", are displayed on the noticeboard of the magnificent St Etheldreda's Church – the oldest Roman Catholic church in Britain, where Sunday Mass is still conducted in Latin, halfway up the street.

One of London's best-kept secrets, Ely Place is a living anachronism from the sixteenth century, when the influential bishops were determined to remain in their Cambridgeshire diocese even while on ministerial missions in the capital. They bought the land in Holborn, then in the outskirts of London, built a palace on it and declared it part of their native Cambridgeshire, so they could carry out their ministerial functions unhindered. They also started growing strawberries in their gardens and were said to produce the finest in the whole of England. A "Strawberry Fayre" is still held in Ely Place every June. In Shakespeare's *Richard III*, the as-yet-uncrowned Gloucester tells the Bishop of Ely:

> *"My Lord of Ely, when I was last in Holborn,*
> *I saw good strawberries in your garden there.*
> *I do beseech you send for some of them"*

In the lane's own Ye Olde Mitre pub, the second oldest in London after Ye Olde Cheshire Cheese, off Fleet Street, which also features London's smallest pub lounge and whose licensing hours were until fairly recently set by the justices of the Isle of Ely, one can view a stack of recent letters addressed to "Ye Olde Mitre Tavern, Ely Place, Holborn Circus, London, Cambridgeshire".

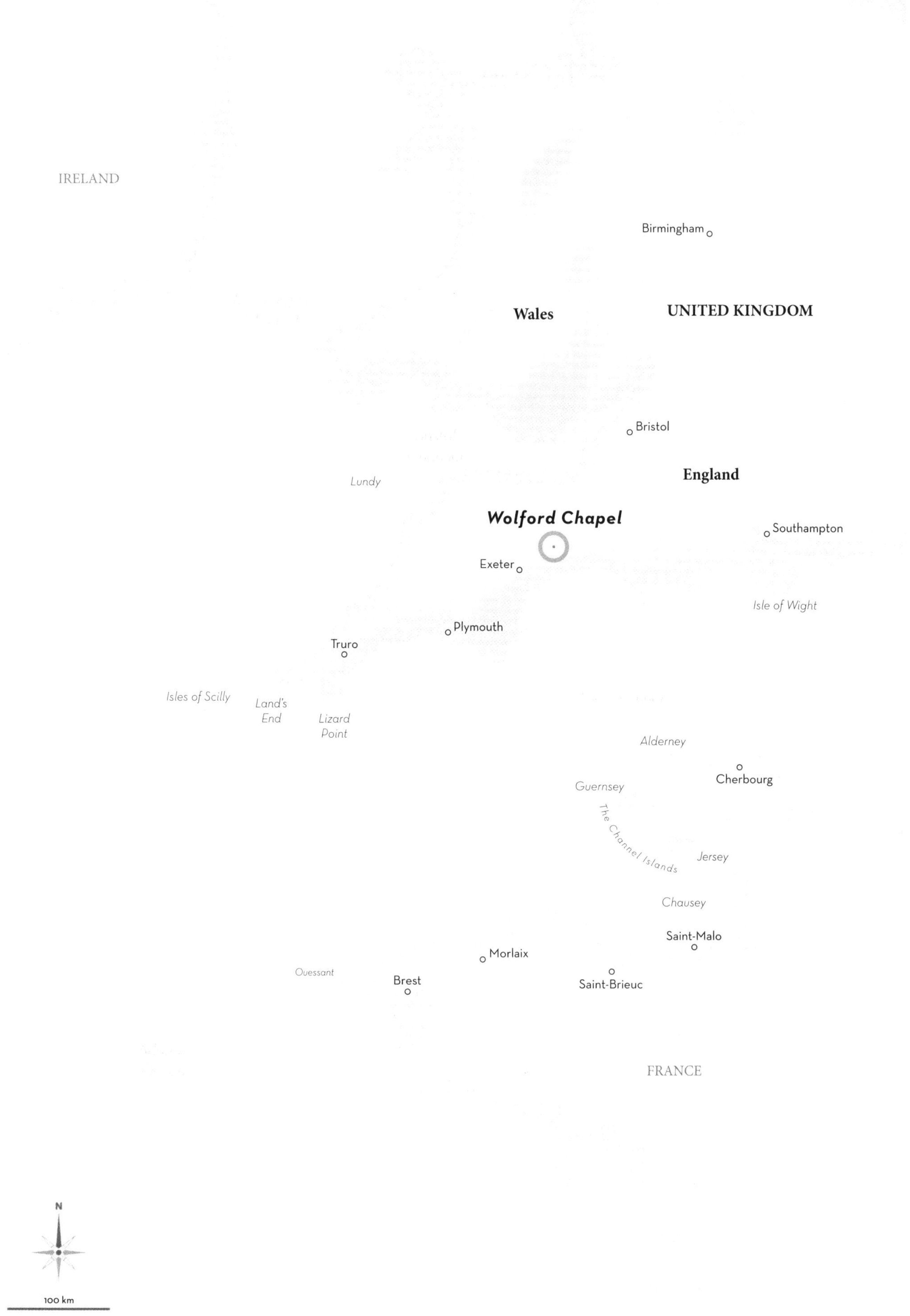

IRELAND

Birmingham ○

Wales   UNITED KINGDOM

○ Bristol

England

Lundy

Wolford Chapel

○ Southampton

Exeter ○

Isle of Wight

○ Plymouth

Truro
○

Isles of Scilly   Land's
End
Lizard
Point

Alderney
○
Cherbourg

Guernsey

The Channel Islands

Jersey

Chausey

Saint-Malo
○

○ Morlaix

Ouessant   Brest   Saint-Brieuc
○   ○

FRANCE

N

100 km

Wolford Chapel · Canada/Great Britain

A chunk of Canada in Devon, England

A piece of Canada in the heart of rural Devon, Wolford Chapel is the burial site of Lord Simcoe, 1st Lieutenant Governor of Upper Canada. Maintained by a local charity, the chapel and the burial grounds around it are, literally, the territory of the Canadian Province of Ontario. A Canadian flag flies above them.

John Graves Simcoe was born at Cotterstock, near Oundle, in 1752, the son of a captain of the Royal Navy. He embarked on a military career and fought in the Revolutionary War, where he was wounded at the siege of Yorktown in 1781.

Simcoe was sent home to England to recuperate and, while convalescing, he met and married an heiress named Elizabeth Gwillim. Elizabeth's money paid for Wolford, a 5,000-acre estate near Honiton where the couple built Wolford Lodge. The lodge remained the Simcoe family's main residence until 1923.

In 1791 Simcoe was placed at the head of British administration in Upper Canada, taking in a territory roughly equivalent to southern Ontario, Lake Superior and Georgian Bay. He held the post for just five years but, during that time, he tried to create a model community based on conservative principles, with an established aristocracy at its head: an idealised version of British law and tradition opposed to the American vision of democracy and Republican ideals south of the border. He founded the city of York, now Toronto, and abolished slavery long before it was abolished in England.

Simcoe later served as Commander in Chief of British forces in India, and died in 1806.

John and Elizabeth Simcoe were buried in the chapel they had built in 1800 near Wolford Lodge, and the couple's children were laid to rest at the chapel near their parents. The chapel and estate were later bought by wealthy publisher Sir Geoffrey Harmsworth.

In 1966, Harmsworth granted the chapel, its historic furnishings and the grounds as a gift to the Ontario Heritage Trust and gave the deed to the chapel to John Robarts, then serving as Premier of the Province of Ontario, making it exterritorial and effectively part of Canada (a virtual temporary enclave), administered and maintained by the trust and the Canadian Embassy in London.

At the same time, a permanent right of way to the property was established across the Simcoe Estate.

A plaque commemorating the gift of Wolford Chapel to the Province of Ontario can still be seen on the chapel's west wall.

© Alison Day at Flickr

IRELAND

Birmingham o

Wales   UNITED KINGDOM

o Bristol

England

Lundy   o Southampton

Exeter o   Isle of Wight

Truro   o Plymouth
  o

Isles of Scilly   Land's
                    End
Bishop Rock ◯   Lizard
                    Point
                                              Alderney

                                                      o
Guernsey   Cherbourg

                    The Channel Islands

                                                Jersey

                                              Chausey

                                          Saint-Malo
                                              o
Ouessant   Morlaix   o
                        o   Saint-Brieuc
            Brest
              o

                                        FRANCE

N

100 km

Bishop Rock · Great Britain

The world's smallest island with a building

The lighthouse-turned-guest house at Bishop Rock, about 6 km west of the Isles of Scilly, can house up to four visitors. The historic 49-metre-tall structure, which was lit by paraffin lamps and candles, now has modern power and even a helipad. It is perched on a small, rocky Atlantic ledge 46 metres long by 16 metres wide, making this the world's smallest island with a building on it, according to the *Guinness Book of Records*.

Bishop Rock is at the eastern end of the North Atlantic shipping route used by ocean liners in the first half of the 20th century; the western end being the entrance to Lower New York Bay. This was the route ocean liners took when competing for the transatlantic speed record, known as the Blue Riband.

The rocks around the Isles of Scilly have wrecked many ships. When Sir Cloudesley Shovell's squadron of the British Fleet sank in 1707 along with at least 1,300 men, the Elder Brethren of Trinity House decided the lighting off the Isles of Scilly was inadequate. They resolved to build a lighthouse on the most westerly danger: the Bishop Rock.

So, in 1847, it was decided to build a screw-pile lighthouse at a cost of £12,000. The first task was to sink cast-iron legs into the solid granite, braced and stayed with wrought-iron rods. Engineer-in-chief James Walker's idea was that the waves would crash through the piles instead of slamming into a solid masonry tower. Within two years it was complete, apart from lighting apparatus. But, the following season, a heavy gale swept away the whole structure on 5 February 1850.

Walker shrugged off the news and turned to the idea of a granite tower. It was a dangerous task, because the sea was rough and the island too small. The workmen had to be housed on a nearby, barren islet, where living quarters and workshops were built. The men were carried to and from the site as the weather permitted. All the granite was brought from the mainland to the islet depot, where it was shaped and numbered before being sent to the rock. After seven years, the tower was completed in 1858.

Bishop Rock was converted to automatic operation in 1991 and the last keepers left the lighthouse in December 1992.

The lighthouse is now controlled from Trinity House's Planning Centre in Harwich, Essex.

IRELAND

Birmingham o

Wales   UNITED KINGDOM

                              o Bristol

Lundy   England

                                        o Southampton

                    Exeter o
                                        Isle of Wight

                          o Plymouth
        Truro
          o

Isles of Scilly   Land's   Lizard
                  End   Point

                                    Alderney
                                              o
                              Guernsey   *Sark*   o Cherbourg
                                         o
                                The
                                  Channel
                                    Islands   Jersey

                                        Chausey

                                              Saint-Malo
                                                   o
                              o Morlaix
        Ouessant   o
                    Brest   Saint-Brieuc
                     o

                                    FRANCE

N

100 km

Sark · Great Britain

The world's last feudal state

The island of Sark, like all other Channel Islands and the Isle of Man, constitutes a part of Great Britain outside the United Kingdom. None of those islands was ever part of the EU.

Not part of the UK, Sark (5.45 sq km, population 500) is the Commonwealth's smallest semi-independent state. It makes its own laws and manages its own money.

Administered by the Seigneur, a hereditary ruler who held the island for the British crown, Sark was the last feudal community in the Western world until 2008, when the islanders voted for democracy and the Seigneur's powers were cut.

The Seigneur, however, still pays an inflation-free tax to the Queen of £1.79 a year. That was obviously a fortune 500 years ago when it first came into force and constituted "one twentieth part of a knight's fee".

Cars are banned from Sark and planes are not allowed to land there or to fly over the island under 2,000 feet. The place is engulfed by a strange quiet, broken only by the wailing of wind.

The island still abides by medieval laws, one of which says that "unspayed bitches are not allowed to be kept on the Island, except by the Seigneur". This law was adopted in the seventeenth century, when Chief Pleas (the island's parliament) decided that too many dogs could cause problems with sheep farming.

Another law states that 40 local family heads, including the Seigneur, are obliged to keep muskets to protect the island from invaders.

A modest-looking brochure (*Constitution of Sark*), written by the island's former Seigneur Michael Beaumont, states that, under Norman custom, a person can obtain immediate cessation of any action he thinks is an infringement of his rights. At the scene, he must, in front of witnesses, recite the Lord's Prayer in French and cry out in *patois*: "*Haro, Haro, Haro! À mon aide, mon Prince, on me fait tort!*" At which point, all actions must cease until the matter is heard by the court.

During World War II, when Sark was occupied by a garrison of 300 Germans, not a single shot was fired from either side and locals still refer to it as a "model occupation". Once, the German commandant of Sark refused to take any action against locals who defied the occupation authorities by keeping short-wave radios at their homes, which was an offence punishable by death anywhere else in occupied Europe.

Exempt from the UK's ailing social security and health schemes, the island takes good care of itself. Special community funds help young people through schools and universities, pay medical bills and provide pensions for the old.

The spot of the last French invasion of Britain (in 1989)

In 1989 the island experienced another foreign invasion, albeit on a much smaller scale, when it was taken over by a drunken Frenchman. André Gards landed on Sark with a rifle and a small load of explosives. In a 'manifesto', written in broken English and pinned on the village noticeboard, he announced he was taking control of the island. Having stated his intentions, he retired for a refill to a village pub, where he was apprehended and disarmed by the constable (head of Sark's part-time police force) and frogmarched to the island's miniature prison – one small windowless cell.

The constable soon came to regret his bravery, for another island law made him responsible for feeding prison inmates and the Frenchman proved to be extremely hungry. Luckily, two days is the maximum jail term in Sark, and the gluttonous invader was deported.

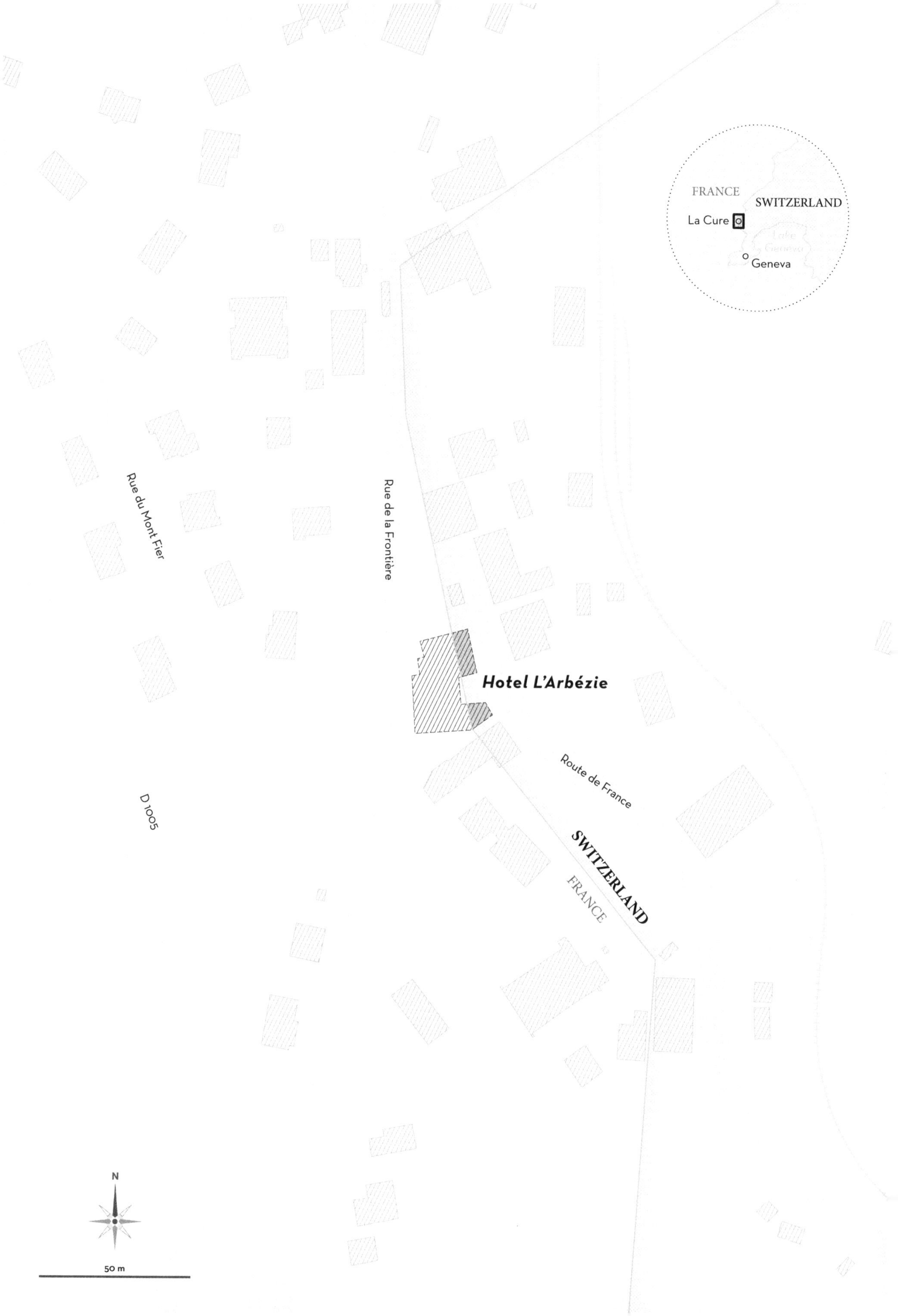

FRANCE   SWITZERLAND

La Cure

Geneva

Rue du Mont Fier

Rue de la Frontière

Hotel L'Arbézie

Route de France

SWITZERLAND

FRANCE

D 1005

N

50 m

Hotel L'Arbézie · France/Switzerland

The world's only hotel straddling an international border where newly-weds could spend their honeymoon night in different countries

The Hotel L'Arbézie is a small two-star hotel in the quiet border town of La Cure (population 2,020), five miles north of Geneva. It is a nice, cosy little place, built in the nineteenth century in alpine style, with wooden beams and a country kitchen. Located a thousand feet above sea level, it is a popular resting place for hikers and skiers.

The hotel looks normal but is unique: it is located exactly on the border between France and Switzerland and is, as far as we know, the only hotel on this planet to do so.

The hotel's history dates back to 8 December 1862, when the Swiss and French governments agreed to a modifica- tion of the border in the Valley of the Dappes. The text of the treaty, named after the valley, stated that no building existing at the time of ratification would be affected by the modification of the border. Clever businessman Monsieur Ponthus seized the opportunity by erecting a building which was on both sides of the new border, intending to do cross-border business.

The structure was put up in record time. When the treaty was ratified by the Swiss government in February 1863, the three-storey building was complete, so not affected by the new border. Ponthus opened a bar on the French side and a shop in Switzerland. The store was there until 1921 when Jules-Jean Arbeze bought the building and turned it into the Franco-Swiss hotel that stands now.

The exceptional location of the hotel has produced a few curious stories. During World War II, France was occupied by Nazi Germany, while Switzerland remained neutral. German soldiers could enter the hotel, but only the part on French soil. To access the upper floors it was necessary to climb a ladder, but the ladder started in Swiss territory, so the upper floors became a refuge for fugitives and the resistance.

In 1962, towards the end of the Algerian War of Independence when a neutral place was needed to sign the Evian agreements, Hotel L'Arbézie Franco-Suisse was chosen for the historic negotiation. A resistance cell was installed on the top floor, dedicated to protecting the threatened and persecuted.

Today, the Franco-Swiss border passes through the kitchen, dining room, hallway and several rooms, continuing to a ski shop at the rear.

The current hotel layout is roughly as follows: the dining room is divided by the boundary, the bar entirely in France, though the boundary passes just outside its front door. Half the bed in the honeymoon suite is in France and the other half in Switzerland. The main hall and stairway are bisected by the border. The lower half of the stairs is in France, the upper half in Switzerland. Another room has its bathroom in France, while the rest of the room is in Switzerland. The annex to the hotel is entirely in Switzerland.

These days, the Hotel L'Arbézie is operated by the French company SARL L'Arbézie Franco-Suisse, which pays taxes to both countries. When the French government banned smoking in French pubs and restaurants in 2008, the rule applied on the Swiss and French sides of the dining room.

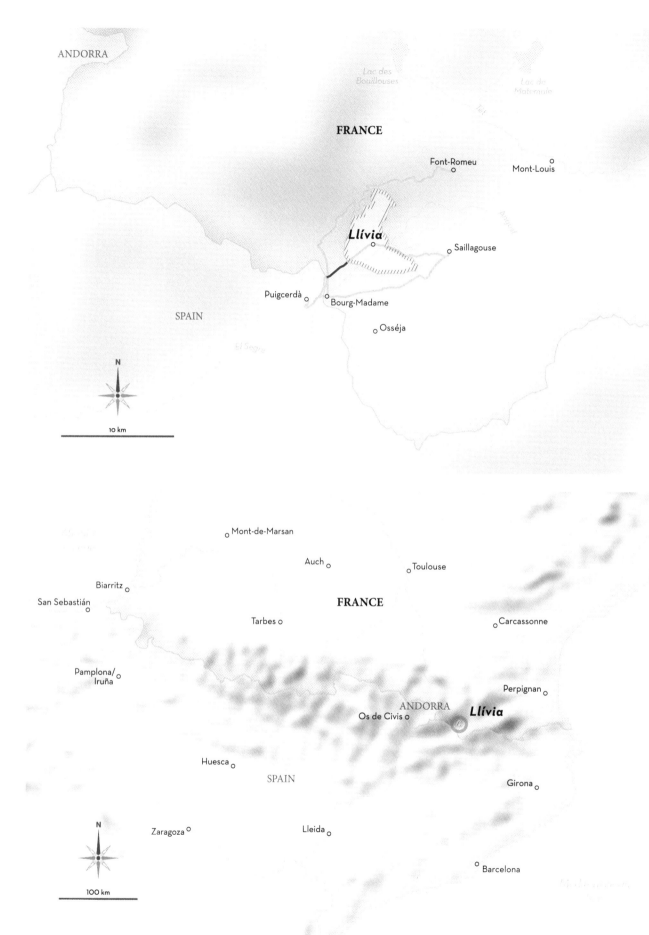

Llívia · France/Spain

-

A misunderstanding made the "village" Spanish,
and loyal locals are determined to keep it that way

Founded by ancient Romans, the town of Llívia (population 1,450) in the foothills of the Pyrenees had been a pawn in Franco-Spanish struggles until the Peace of the Pyrenees treaty in 1659 (ending an 11-year war between the two nations) gave 33 "villages" in the Cerdagne plain to Louis XIV of France.

The French thought Llívia was included in the transfer, but the Spanish regarded the territory not as a village (*pueblo*), but a town (*villa*). Having spotted the discrepancy, the patriotic residents of Llívia, who wanted to remain Spanish, claimed the treaty had nothing to do with them and the French had to agree. So the enclave status of Llívia was the result of a misunderstanding of the definition of "village".

Before the euro was introduced in 1992, French francs and Spanish pesetas were freely circulated in Llívia. According to some locals, due to ridiculous bureaucratic regulations in the pre-internet age, a letter from a nearby French village a couple of miles away took 15 days to arrive, and to call the same French village from Llívia required an international code.

With the euro now in circulation, prices in Llívia remain much lower than those in France. As a result, French villagers are shopping there in growing numbers and Llívia's relations with its French neighbours have improved to the point that it shares a hospital with France. Some other municipal services are also jointly administered and funded by both countries.

And yet, modern Llívia remains fiercely Catalan, with the Catalan flag flying from the roofs of most houses and very few people willing to speak French to a visitor – unusual for a "town" surrounded by France. In Llívia, it is hard to buy a bottle of French wine, and only one per cent of the town's permanent population are French citizens. On the day of the Catalonia independence referendum of 2019, when Spain shut down internet across the province, Llívia's mayor decided to use the French internet connection so the vote could proceed. They even took the ballots to France to have them counted, just in case.

What also strikes the visitor to Llívia is the proliferation of pharmacies, selling all sorts of herbal cures made from Pyrenean plants and wild flowers – Llívia's main industry. Characteristically, the town's most popular attraction is a pharmacy: *Farmacia de Esteva*, founded in 1594 and advertising itself as "Europe's oldest".

Whether the latter is true or not, Llívia, which was disdainfully characterised by guidebook author Karl Baedeker as "a dirty village of ancient origin with some ruins remaining" in his Southern France travel guide, is now spotlessly clean and reassuringly healthy.

Today, Llívia is linked to Spain by a 4 km 'neutral road' without customs control.

Pointe Sainte-Anne

Hondarribia ○

○ Hendaye

SPAIN

FRANCE

Île aux Faisans

Irun ○

Bidassoa

N

2 km

○ Mont-de-Marsan

Auch ○

○ Toulouse

Biarritz ○

San Sebastián ○ Île aux Faisans

FRANCE

Tarbes ○

○ Carcassonne

Pamplona/ ○
Iruña

ANDORRA

Perpignan ○

Os de Civis ○

Huesca ○

SPAIN

Girona ○

N

Zaragoza ○

Lleida ○

○ Barcelona

100 km

Pheasant Island · France/Spain

Unique in the world:

an island that changes owners every six months

Pheasant Island (aka Conference Island) covers 3,000 square metres, in the centre of the Bidasoa river, bordering France and Spain. No one seems to know how the island got its name as only ducks – no pheasants – have ever been sighted there.

From a purely legal point of view, since the 1856 Treaty of Bayonne – which decreed by a convention in 1901 that Pheasant Island was a condominium that would be jointly governed by France and Spain – its sovereignty has switched hands every six months.

It is the only example in contemporary international relations of sovereignty alternating on a single territory – from 1 August to 31 January for France and from 1 February to 31 July for Spain.

The condominium is governed by two viceroys. The French viceroy has been the naval commander in Bordeaux since the Ardour naval base in Bayonne closed in July 2015. The writer Pierre Loti was one of these viceroys.

On the Spanish side, the viceroy is the commander of the naval base of Hondarribia and of San Sebastian.

On 1 February 2012, for the first time, a ceremony was held on the island to mark the transfer of power between the two viceroys.

The island can no longer be visited today but can easily be observed from the la *rive des Joncaux*, on the *Chemin de la Baie* (Hendaye).

This tiny island has witnessed extraordinary events. In 1526 in a boat off the island, Francis I, who had been taken prisoner in Spain the year before, was freed in exchange for his two sons, who were held as hostages instead.

In 1615 the French and Spanish ambassadors met to exchange two royal fiancées: Isabelle, daughter of Henry IV, king of France, was promised in marriage to Philip IV, and her sister, Anne of Austria, betrothed to Louis XIII.

In 1659, King Louis XIV met the King of Castille there to sign the Treaty of the Pyrenees which would put an end to a long war between France and Spain, and in June 1660, Louis XIV's marriage to Mary-Theresa of Austria, the daughter of King Philip IV, was sealed. A monument in commemoration of the 1659 conference was built on the island in 1861 by the two neighbouring countries.

On 4 December 1904, Paul Déroulède and Jean Jaurès fought each other just opposite the island, after Jaurès published an ironic article in his newspaper, *L'Humanité*. Déroulède, a nationalist deputy, is quoted as having quipped to Jaurès, when he was the leader of the socialist party: "You are the most offensive perverter of consciences, in France, ever to have played into the hands of foreigners." Their pistol duel ended in a draw. A few years later, on 31 July 1914, it was indeed a pistol (belonging to Raoul Villain) that ended Jaurès' life, at the *Café Croissant* in Paris (see the guide *Secret Paris* by the same editor).

On 23 October 1940, a meeting was arranged on Pheasant Island between Adolf Hitler and General Francisco Franco. Legend has it that Franco kept the Führer waiting for more than 30 minutes, but historians say eight minutes. During the meeting, Franco confirmed Spain's refusal to join forces with Germany, which proved pivotal in World War II.

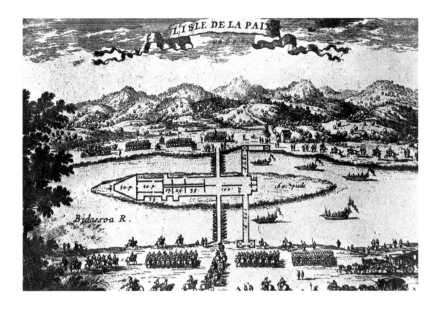

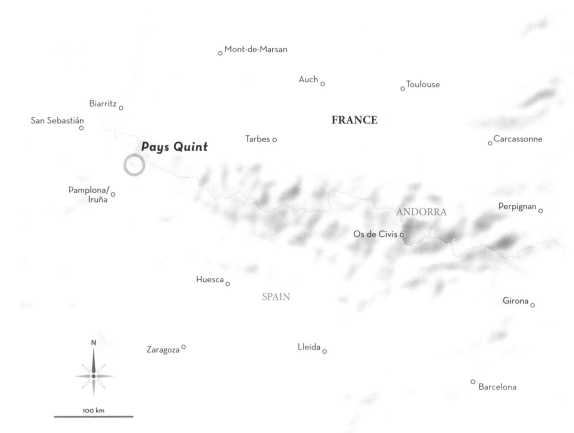

Mont-de-Marsan

Auch   Toulouse

Biarritz

San Sebastián

Pays Quint

FRANCE

Tarbes   Carcassonne

Pamplona/
Iruña

ANDORRA   Perpignan

Os de Civis

Huesca

SPAIN   Girona

N

Zaragoza   Lleida

Barcelona

100 km

Pays Quint · France/Spain

A Spanish territory administered by France

Also called Quintoa in Basque or Quinto Real in Spanish, Pays Quint is a territory on the Franco–Spanish border, south of the Aldudes Valley in the French Basque region. Its northern part belongs to Spain but it is administered by France, which pays an annual rent to exert this right. That explains why, on maps, it is considered a French possession.

'Quint' derives from the 'right of quint', created in 1237, which was historically the 'right for swine to eat acorns'. This right authorised the collection and feeding of acorns to pigs being led to summer pastures in the royal mountains of Navarre, allowing the royal authorities to collect a fifth of the pigs' value in taxes (hence the name 'quint').

In the fourteenth century, the Independent Kingdom of Navarre straddled the Pyrenees. The communes of Baïgorry (to the north) and the Erro and Baztan Valleys (to the south) lived, more or less, peacefully together. Rare conflicts were swiftly and decisively settled.

In 1512, however, Aragon successfully fought for the possession of the Kingdom of Navarre which was then, rapidly through a game of alliances, integrated into the Kingdom of Spain. The Kingdom of Navarre was subsequently cut in two: Upper Navarre, in the south, was given to Spain. In the north, Lower Navarre remained independent until the day its king, Henry III of Navarre, became the King of France and of Navarre under the name of Henry IV.

Until 1700, the construction of houses was not authorised on this territory. It was the youngest sons of Baïgorry who were to defy this ban when they settled there and went on to create the parishes of Aldudes, Banca and Urepel (the current Northern Pays Quint). Many battles ensued. Excluded from any rights to inheritance by the Basque tradition that ensured all assets and family titles were passed to the eldest man or woman, the youngest sons were destined to become priests, soldiers or fishermen. This partly explains the presence of a large Basque diaspora in South and North America.

After being ignored by the Treaty of the Pyrenees (1659), which set the border between France and Spain according to the principle of the water divide, Pays Quint gained its current status thanks to the Treaty of Bayonne in 1856. The treaty gave the ownership of the entire territory of Pays Quint to Spain (25 sq km), but France was given full rights to use the northern part of the zone (Aldudes, Banca, Urepel) and to graze livestock in the southern part (Erro and Baztan Valleys) in exchange for an annual rent.

The hybrid status of Northern Pays Quint still exists. The French Post Office ensures the distribution of mail, but Spain supplies the electricity and is in charge of security. The administration of the territory is run by the commune of Urepel (France) and the French department of the 'Pyrénées-Atlantique'.

Only about 15 French people now live in this area of Spanish land, where the electricity was installed in 1979 and the telephone lines in 1983. They pay their property taxes in Spain, but their residency and income taxes in France. They also send their children to French schools and are entitled to French Family Allowance.

Mont-de-Marsan

Auch   Toulouse

Biarritz

San Sebastián   FRANCE

Tarbes   Carcassonne

Pamplona/
Iruña   ANDORRA   Perpignan

                                                    Os de Civís

Huesca

                    SPAIN   Girona

N

Zaragoza   Lleida

                                                    Barcelona

100 km

Os de Civís · Spain/Andorra

A Spanish village that can only be reached by car through Andorra

Os de Civís is a special Spanish village with rare geography. If travelling by car, it can only be reached from the rest of Spain by driving through Andorra, the country enclaved between France and Spain.

Os de Civís is therefore a rare case of a pene-enclave (practical enclave – see page 7).

As it is an extremely limited point of access, there is no border control when driving between the two countries. That is a unique situation in Andorra, because all the other routes across the border do have one, as Andorra is neither part of the Schengen Area nor a member of the European Union. Os de Civís is almost entirely dependent on Andorra, despite its electrical network being wired up to Spain since 1982. This is because both the Upper and Lower Seturia Valley are in Andorran territory: the only direct link with the neighbouring Spanish Civís Valley is a mountain trail, on foot, which goes through the confluent mountain pass at an altitude of 2,177 metres.

ampione d'Italia · Italy/Switzerland

The Italian town enclaved within Switzerland
is a striking merger of contrasting national traits

Politically Italian, but economically Swiss, Campione d'Italia (2.68 sq km, population 1,900) is an Italian enclave within Switzerland. Its residents vote in Italian elections but are paid in Swiss francs to suit the prices, which are Swiss.

Swiss francs are the currency of the town, where the safeguarding of law and order is entrusted to the Italian police force, with most constables coming from Como. Every time a policeman goes back home, he has to leave his weapons in Campione – in accordance with a Swiss law forbidding foreigners to carry arms in Switzerland.

The Campionese drive cars with "TI" number plates – for Ticino, the Swiss canton by which it is surrounded – but mail their letters with stamps of the Italian Republic. They have a choice of Swiss or Italian postcodes, with most preferring the former over the notoriously slow and unreliable Italian postal service. They shop for food in Switzerland, where they have unhindered, passport-free access, and for clothes in Italy, where Italian border guards routinely check their Italian passports.

Although part of Italy, Campione is nevertheless not part of the EU. Despite this, Campione's residents – as Italian passport holders – have the right to live and work in any EU member state, but not in Switzerland, on whose territory the town is located.

Campione is part of the European Union Customs Territory, but not of the EU per se, for Campione's tax rates remain those of Switzerland, which are much lower than in Italy.

Campione's striking duality started in 777 AD, when local landowner Totone tried to buy himself an indulgence for his sins by donating all his holdings, including the small fishing village of Campione, then part of the diocese of Como, to the Basilica of St Ambrose in Milan. As a result, Campione fell under the rule of the Milanese ecclesiastical authorities, and not those of nearby Como, as would have been more logical. Throughout the Middle Ages, while the Abbot of St Ambrose had spiritual control over Campione, the village's everyday affairs were greatly influenced by the Swiss region of Lugano.

This ambivalence went on until the Swiss obtained full possession of the region comprising the present-day canton of Ticino in 1512. With Campione remaining an outlier of Milan, it became a full-scale enclave within Switzerland. The Swiss made numerous peaceful attempts to gain control of Campione, but failed. Shortly after the village was annexed to the new Kingdom of Italy in 1861, an international convention to specify Campione's boundaries came into force, sealing the enclave's fate.

This small Italian town strikes an accidental visitor as un-Italian or Swiss-like in its cleanliness, the absence of washing on balconies and the quiet demeanour of the locals, who seldom raise their voices. It is as if two seemingly incompatible lifestyles and national characteristics have been recycled and neatly packed into less than three square kilometres of its territory.

In the words of the Italian writer Giovanni Cenzato, Campione remains "a little Italian boy wearing a Swiss costume".

AUSTRIA

o Vaduz

LIECHTENSTEIN

o Chur

o Davos

SWITZERLAND

Zermez o

Munt la Schera Tunnel

3 093 m ▲

▲ 2 784 m

Livigno

Engadina

3 090 m ▲

Foscagno Pass

Saint Moritz o

▲ 2 291 m

o Bormio

2 315 m

Forcola di Livigno

▲ 3 182 m

Valtellina

Poschiavo o

o Tirano

Locarno o

Sondrio o

Morbegno o

Lugano o

ITALY

Lake Maggiore

Lake Como

Lecco o

Varese o

Como o

Lake Iseo

Brescia o

N

o Milano

Lake Garda

50 km

Livigno · Italy

*A duty-free valley in the Italian Alps, not a member of the EU,
with the right to moor its non-existent vessels in the Black Sea ports*

Livigno (population 5,000) – a 13-kilometre-long Alpine valley in the Italian province of Sondrio – is a duty-free area, excluded from EU membership by a special protocol: Italian VAT is not paid.

People outside Livigno go there to buy goods but within certain limits strictly enforced by local authorities and Italian customs (a 10-packet carton of cigarettes or 4 litres of wine, for instance). Buying petrol is also much cheaper, although you are only allowed to fill your tank plus one jerrican of up to 10 litres.

Tax advantages for Livigno were recorded as far back as the sixteenth century (and in the early seventeenth century, the valley even enjoyed a short period of complete independence, when ruled by the Grigioni family) and it was given customs benefits by Napoleon, which were later confirmed by the Austro-Hungarian Empire in 1818. They were confirmed by the Kingdom of Italy around 1910, and the Italian Republic and the European Economic Community in 1960. Although no VAT is paid, income taxes are, so Livigno cannot be considered a tax haven.

The justification for such a status is the difficulty in reaching Livigno during winter, and the centuries-long history of poverty in the region. Until the winter of 1952–1953, when the first road that could be used in winter was built from Switzerland (under the protection of Italy's Minister of Finance, a native of neighbouring Valtellina), Livigno was completely cut off from the rest of the world until spring. Still today, the Foscagno Pass inaugurated in 1914 is the only road access to Livigno from Italy.

Various states, and finally Italy, wanted with this measure to ensure people would have an incentive to live in the area, so they could claim it territorially. At the same time, the tax revenue from Livigno would have been negligible anyway.

Only three roads lead to the town. Two link to Switzerland, one through the Forcola di Livigno, elevation 2,315 metres and open in summer only, and the second through the Munt la Schera Tunnel. The third connects to other parts of Italy at an elevation of 2,291 metres.

Leaving Livigno for the rest of Italy, there is a customs checkpoint on the road.

The valley also has its own language. Yes, language – not just a dialect. Unlike other Sondrio dialects (Bormino, Tiranese, etc.), Livignasc incorporates lots of Romansch, Spanish and German words, and therefore cannot be understood in other parts of Italy. It is different enough to justify an Italian–Livignasc Dictionary, the first and so far only edition of which has been put together by a group of local enthusiasts.

With all its hotels and duty-free shops, Livigno can be safely regarded as the hub of commercialism in the Retiche Alps. All shops are open from morning until late at night (with a two-hour lunch break), seven days a week, 365 days a year. Some time ago, a devout Roman Catholic wanted to close her store on Sundays, but Livigno authorities refused. Duty-free obviously came before religious (or any other) duty in Livigno, where shops employ over 3,000 people – more than half the residents.

Located high in the Retiche Alps, between the valleys of Valtellina and Engadina, Livigno, alongside several other Italian villages, is officially and surprisingly (we did not find out why yet) part of the Danube Basin economic area. This means it enjoys the right of free mooring in the Black Sea ports – but it has no maritime vessels.

The Order of Malta · Italy

The only private organisation in the world with privileges normally given to a country: extraterritoriality, embassies …

The Sovereign military hospitaller Order of Saint John of Jerusalem, of Rhodes and of Malta, or, depending on the period in history, more commonly known as order of the Hospital, Hospitaller order, order of Rhodes, or order of Malta, is one of the oldest Catholic orders. Its mission is to defend the faith and take care of the needy and the sick. It was created in Jerusalem in the second half of the eleventh century by merchants of the former Amalfi Republic to assist pilgrims in the Holy Land. This monastic community is dedicated to Saint John the Baptist and was recognised as a religious order by pope Pascal II in 1113.

Following the capture of Jerusalem after the 1099 crusades, it also rapidly became a military order, a few years before the Knights Templar settled there. After losing Jerusalem and Saint John of Acre in 1291, the order retreated to Cyprus and remained there from 1291 to 1309. Due to growing rivalry with the king of Cyprus, the order conquered the Island of Rhodes, which was then under Byzantine rule, and set up its new headquarters there in 1310, which lasted until 1523.

Due to its insular nature, the order built up a fleet that would establish its reputation. After being defeated by the Turks, it moved to Civitavecchia and then to Viterbo, in Italy, before going to Nice and finally settling in Malta in 1530, with the blessing of Charles V, who understood that its presence would help him ward off Ottoman offensives. Napoleon drove the order out in 1798 and, finally, the pope allowed it to settle in Rome in 1834.

Before the loss of Malta, the order was mostly comprised of religious members who had taken the three vows of poverty, chastity and obedience. Today, although some of its members are monks, most of them are secular knights and ladies (currently over 12,500). The order has not played a military role since 1798.

Initially knights of the order had to be from noble and knightly Christian families, but now members who distinguish themselves by their faith, moral values and merits in the eyes of the Church and the order itself are admitted. Although volunteers are always welcome, formal applications are not permitted.

The order maintains diplomatic relations with 104 countries through its embassies. It has a very special status, as it is the only private organisation to be practically treated as a country in its own right.

Its activities are funded from donations by members, private donations and income from its properties.

In Rome, the order possesses two headquarters which enjoy extraterritorial status: the palace of Malta, at n° 68 Via dei Condotti, home of the Grand Master where governmental bodies meet, and the Villa Malta in the district of Aventin, where the Grand Priory of Rome, the embassy of the order of the Holy Seat and the embassy of Italy have their headquarters.

SWITZERLAND

Milan

Venice

SLOVENIA

HUNGARY

CROATIA

FRANCE

San Marino

BOSNIA AND
HERZEGOVINA

SERBIA

ITALY

MONTENEGRO

Kosovo

Rome

NORTH
MACEDONIA

Naples

ALBANIA

GREECE

N

200 km

San Marino

An enclaved mini-state and the world's oldest republic

Fully surrounded by north-central Italy, San Marino (61 sq km; population 33,000) is an enclaved microstate officially recognised by the UN. It is the world's oldest republic, founded in the fourth century AD.

With a well-deserved reputation of being a haven of peace and liberty, during World War II it opened its borders to more than 100,000 refugees from Nazi-occupied countries.

Modern San Marino has one of the world's most confusing and, proportionally, largest governmental and judicial bureaucracies.

The microstate has three separate, voluntary armies: the Territorial Army, the Fortification Guards and the Noble Guards, not to mention its traditional Crossbow Corps. San Marino has a zero crime rate and one prison of just four cells (but also with a gym, private library and a TV room), but has two police forces – the gendarmerie and the civil police.

The republic's ruling hierarchy, modestly calling itself 'Serenissima'(Most Serene)', probably to imitate the Venetian Republic, seems cumbersome to the point of madness. It is made up of six bodies: the Arengo, the Grand and General Council, the Captains Regent, the Council of the Twelve, the Sindaci (high officials) and the State Congress.

The Arengo, or the assembly of the heads of families, used to be the country's parliament. Now it has only one, vague, function: the right of petition.

The 60-seat Grand and General Council, San Marino's highest legislative body, nominates two Captains Regent who jointly rule for six months and then get re-elected. Executive power is wielded by the State Congress, composed of three secretaries and seven ministers, among them the minister for culture and universities.

The Council of the Twelve's main role is "to authorise the sale and transfer of dowry possessions by the wife". As to the mysterious Sindaci, it is just the body of government inspectors representing the state.

There is also the Castle Board, presided over by the Captain of the Castles and comprising delegates of San Marino's nine districts (Castles).

With 25 per cent of the population employed in "public administration", the structure of the judicial system is no less complicated. Unfortunately, or perhaps fortunately, we do not have enough space to describe it here. One thing is certain: it is very hard to decide who is in charge of what in San Marino …

There are only two other fully enclaved countries in the world (having no access either to a sea or to a major lake or river): the Vatican and Lesotho.

Gorizia-Transalpina Square/ Nova Gorica, Europe Square · Italy/Slovenia

The world's only town square divided by an international border
and the scene of one of the most bizarre checkpoint protests

South-east of Udine and north-west of Trieste, the border between Italy and Slovenia goes crazy. Separating the Italian city of Gorizia and the Slovenian city of Nova Gorica, it splits the town's main square down the middle and forms a peculiar public space called Europe Square on the Slovenian side and Transalpina Square in Italy. It is the world's only town square divided by an international border, in accordance with the February 1947 Paris Peace Treaty.

The train station in the middle of the square was completed in 1906, when the whole region of Goriška (*il Goriziano* in Italian) was still part of the Austro-Hungarian empire.

After World War I, according to the Treaty of Rapallo, the whole region of Primorska Litorale was annexed by Italy. When in the course of World War II Italy capitulated (in 1943), the region was occupied by Germany. In May 1945, Yugoslav soldiers entered Gorizia and, from 12 June 1945, the area was divided by a provisional border called the Morgan Line, with Zone A controlled by the Allies and Zone B by Yugoslavs. The town of Gorizia became Italian, and the train station found itself next to it, in Yugoslav territory.

Nova Gorica is a relatively new town, founded in 1948 on the orders of Marshal Tito, then the President of Yugoslavia. It was not until 1980 that, ignoring communist principles, several large casinos were opened. Locals, however, were not allowed to gamble. According to a 1988 Yugoslavian guide to Nova Gorica: "The proximity of the border is stimulating the growth of business in the hotel industry, and the Casino is now one of the features available to visitors from abroad".

Until 1954, the square had been dissected along the frontier line by rows of barbed wire and, later, a concrete fence. After the creation of Slovenia in 1991, all the barriers were partially removed in 2004, when the country joined the EU, and taken away completely in 2011.

The history of that Italian-Slovenian divide is far less sinister than that of the Berlin Wall, yet hundreds of people, mostly from the Yugoslav side, were killed and injured trying to cross the border illegally, particularly in the first several years of its existence between 1947 and 1950.

Then, of course, there were smugglers. Tito's Yugoslavia was much better off in material terms than any other country of the former Communist Bloc. Yet the gap in living standards with neighbouring Italy was striking, so the few lucky Slovenes officially allowed to travel across the border made sure they carried substantial amounts of local produce. They took meat, honey, wine, etc. and brought back manufactured goods: cameras, radios, household items and, later, electronics.

Curiously, ordinary sorghum brooms which, like many other basic household goods were scarce in communist Yugoslavia, swept their way into history in August 1950 when a crowd of nearly 5,000 Slovenes illegally crossed the border. They were protesting against the checkpoint's temporary closure, which left them unable to buy necessities. The crowds stopped short of trespassing, but staged a peaceful demonstration on the neutral land between the two checkpoints – Slovenian and Italian – and many of them were waving their worn-out brooms. That impromptu gathering became known as The March of the Brooms, or Broom Sunday.

HUNGARY

Mohács

Batina   Bezdan

Beli Manastir

Gornja Siga

Sombor

CROATIA

Apatin

SERBIA

Darda

Osijek

Vukovar

HUNGARY
ROMANIA
CROATIA
BOSNIA
AND
HERZ.
SERBIA

N

10 km

Gornja Siga · Croatia/Serbia

A territory in the heart of Europe unclaimed by any country

After the Yugoslav wars between 1991 and 2001, the Serbia–Croatia border to the north-west of Serbia and north-east of Croatia was defined by the course of the Danube and, more officially, by the current thalweg of the Danube – in other words, the line formed by the points with the lowest altitude in a watercourse.

Changes in the course of the Danube created deep meanderings. Croatia is claiming not the current, but the former thalweg of the Danube as the border, which, of course, has the benefit of giving it more territory.

In the sector of the Danube north of the river, Drave – eight large territories sitting on the east bank, bordered by the former course of the Danube – has been claimed by Croatia, which considers four smaller territories on the West bank to be part of Serbia. Serbia, of course, does not recognise these four small territories, after rejecting the border claimed by Croatia, which would effectively amount to a loss of precious square kilometres. Croatia does not wish to recognise them either, as it would mean losing a chance to negotiate possession of the eight territories on the other bank of the Danube.

This territorial dispute has led to an absurd situation, with neither country recognising these four territories, the largest of which is called Gornja Siga.

In 2015, a Czech named Vít Jedlička took advantage of this situation by creating a micro-state in Gornja Siga which he named Liberland. For once, Serbia and Croatia agreed: Liberland was nothing more than an amusing joke limited within the confines of international law. Officially, Gornja Siga belongs to no country.

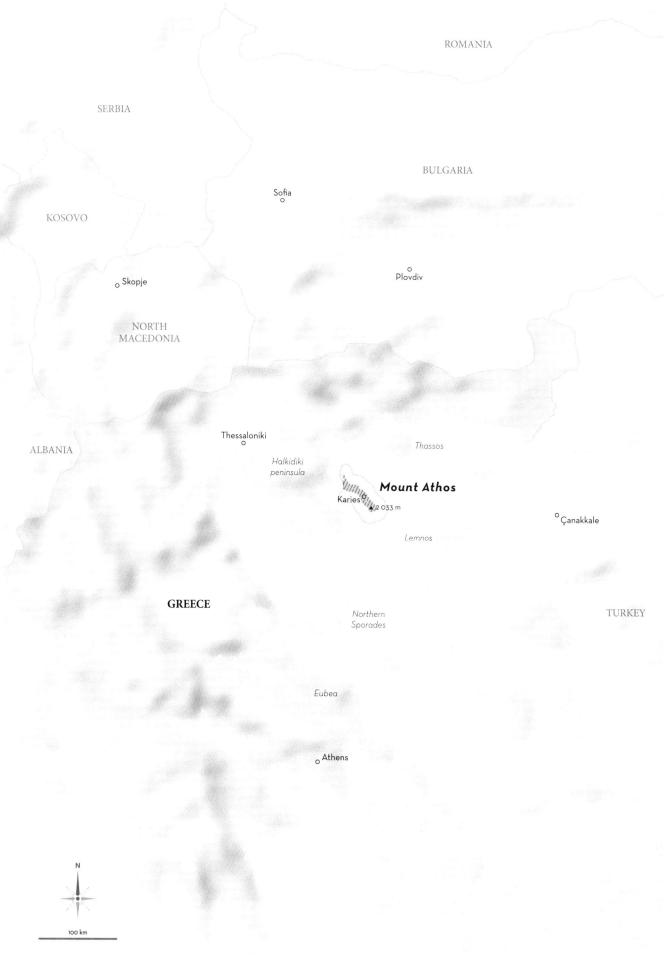

ROMANIA

SERBIA

BULGARIA

Sofia

KOSOVO

Skopje

Plovdiv

NORTH
MACEDONIA

Thessaloniki

Thassos

ALBANIA

*Halkidiki
peninsula*

Mount Athos

Karies

2 033 m

Çanakkale

Lemnos

GREECE

TURKEY

*Northern
Sporades*

Eubea

Athens

N

100 km

Mount Athos · Greece

A unique semi-independent Orthodox monastic state, separated from Greece by a wall, where only men and male animals are allowed

Mount Athos, also called the Holy Mountain, is a semi-independent Orthodox monastic state on the Halkidiki peninsula in northern Greece. It is one of the world's most spiritual places, where monks spend their lives in prayer and contemplation. To go there, a foreigner has to receive a '*Diamonitirion*' – an entry permit limited to 10 per day for non-Orthodox persons (to be applied for by email).

The Holy Mountain can only be accessed from the sea, by boat or ferry. A wall separates Mount Athos from the rest of Greece.

The earliest records suggest the first hermits, seeking refuge from the iconoclast emperors, came to Mount Athos in the eighth century. In 1060, a monastic republic was established there as a self-administered area of Greece. Today, some 2,500 monks and hermits live there in 20 monasteries (17 Greek, one Russian, one Bulgarian and one Serbian) and lots of smaller ones – abbeys, *sketes*, cells and huts – all under the direct jurisdiction of the Ecumenical Patriarch of Constantinople. Each larger monastery resembles a fortified medieval town, with turrets, moats and thick stone walls.

Officially, a visitor is allowed to stay only one night in each monastery. The next day, they have to walk to the next monastery. Monasteries offer a bed, breakfast and dinner for free, although donations are welcome. There is no lunch offered and no restaurant outside the 'capital' at Karies, close to where the boat arrives.

Most of the monasteries also possess unique artistic and historical treasures that are sometimes shown to visitors upon request or during masses.

A trip to Mount Athos (officially restricted to five days, but visa extensions are not very hard to get) is a unique experience. Apart from the beautiful nature (although large dirt roads have been built recently in many places) and the exceptional architecture of the monasteries (some were built in medieval times, others in the sixteenth or seventeenth centuries), it is above all a spiritual experience.

Mount Athos has the other major distinction of remaining firmly closed to females, be they human or animal. Only a couple of monks have special permits to keep hens, whose eggs they use for mixing paints. This unique local law is tirelessly enforced by the mountain state's monastic police force – the Serdaris. From the year 1006, no 'smooth-faced person' has been allowed on its shores. Even the Queen of England, on a visit to Greece, had to admire the monasteries from the sea, at least 500 yards from the shore.

There have been several cases of women, driven by curiosity, getting to the Holy Mountain dressed as men. In each case, the trespassers were discovered and sent back to the mainland by the *Serdaris*. The last recorded female "intrusion" was in 2008, when four Moldavian women were abandoned on Mount Athos by human traffickers.

The most remarkable, however, goes back to 1930, when Alice Diplarakou, who had recently won the title of Miss Europe (the first ever Greek contestant to win it), got ashore in Mount Athos and spent a couple of days there. One of the monks of the monastery where she stayed fell head over heels in love. Having broken his vows, he followed her to Athens and asked her to marry him, only to find out she was already married. On hearing the news, the poor monk went insane and finished his days in a psychiatric hospital. He never saw the Holy Mountain again.

In 1997, an exhibition of the artistic treasures of the Holy Mountain (priceless icons and frescoes, Ptolemy's first map of the world, etc.) was held in Salonika. It was the first attempt on the part of the monks to establish closer contacts with the outside world. Titillated by the unspeakable treasures on display, a group of feminists filed a suit in the European Court of Human Rights demanding to rescind the male-only status of the Holy Mountain. The suit was thrown out.

TURKEY

SYRIA

Yialousa ○   *Karpas Peninsula*

Kyrenia ○   **Turkish Republic of Northern Cyprus**

Morphou Bay

Kokkina   ■ **Nicosia**   ○ Famagusta

CYPRUS

Toodros Mountains   Larnaca ○

Republic of Cyprus

Paphos ○   Limassol ○

N

50 km

LEBANON

Kokkina · Cyprus

A heavily contested ghost exclave/enclave in Cyprus,
now populated only by the military

Kokkina (Greek: Κόκκινα, Turkish: Erenköy), civilian population 0, is a village in Cyprus administered by the internationally unrecognised Turkish Republic of Northern Cyprus (TRNC), of which it is now a coastal exclave. Hemmed in on three sides by mountainous territory, controlled by the Republic of Cyprus, with the Mediterranean Sea (Morphou Bay) on its northern flank, the exclave sits several kilometres away from what constitutes the main area of the TRNC.

After 1960, when Cyprus got its independence from Britain (which kept two military bases in the south, see page 103), the new country was divided between a Turkish minority (18 per cent of the population) and a Greek majority (82 per cent). The rise of a nationalistic movement in Greece, aimed at the unification of Cyprus and Greece, led to the intense confrontation between the Greek Cypriot and Turkish Cypriot communities during the inter-communal struggle of 1963–1964.

In July 1974, after an attempted coup by nationalistic generals in Greece in favour of the unification of Cyprus with Greece, Turkey decided to invade northern Cyprus, claiming the right to protect the Turkish Cypriot population. Within two days it occupied the northern part of the country (38 per cent of the territory), with 200,000 Greek Cypriots forced to leave northern Cyprus and 50,000 Turkish Cypriots moved there.

A separate Turkish Cypriot state was established in the north by unilateral declaration in 1983. The move was widely condemned by the international community, with the new state being recognised only by Turkey, which sent some Turkish settlers from Anatolia to populate northern Cyprus in another move condemned by the UN. Today, about 23 per cent of the population of Cyprus is Turkish.

After heavy fighting in 1964, some Turkish Cypriots gathered in north-west Cyprus, in the area of Kokkina. This area became an official Turkish exclave when the Turkish military invaded Cyprus in 1974 and declared independence in 1984.

In 1976, all Kokkina inhabitants were transferred to Gialousa, a town on Cyprus' Karpas Peninsula later renamed Yeni Erenköy (New Erenköy). The exclave of Kokkina has since functioned as a North Cyprus Defence Force military camp.

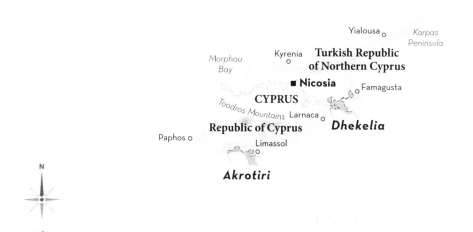

TURKEY

SYRIA

Yialousa ○   Karpas
                    Peninsula

Morphou   Kyrenia   **Turkish Republic**
Bay   ○   **of Northern Cyprus**

            ■ **Nicosia**
                              Famagusta
CYPRUS   ●

Toodros Mountains Larnaca ○   *Dhekelia*

Republic of Cyprus

Paphos ○

            Limassol
            ○

Akrotiri

N

50 km

Republic of Cyprus

Episkopi
○   Limassol
Trachoni ○   ○

Akrotiri

○ Akrotiri

Cape   Cape
Zevgari   Gata

N

5 km

**Turkish Republic
of Northern Cyprus**   Famagusta ○

Lysi   Ayios
○   Nikolaos ○

                    Avgorou   Phrenaros
                    ○   ○
Xylotymvou   Sotira ○
○   *Dhekelia*
                    Ormideia   Liopetri
                    ○   ○
Oroklini   **Republic of Cyprus**
○
            Dhekelia   Xylofagou
            Power Station   ○

N

5 km

Akrotiri and Dhekelia ·
Great Britain/Cyprus

A forgotten part of the UK within Cyprus,
with the euro, not the pound, in circulation

The British Sovereign Base Areas of Akrotiri and Dhekelia (population 14,000, area 254 sq km) comprise those parts of Cyprus which stayed under British jurisdiction and remained British sovereign territory when the 1960 Treaty of Establishment created the independent Republic of Cyprus.

They constitute a semi-independent British Overseas Territory, governed by the Administrator, who is also the Commander of the Armed Forces.

The bases remain formally a part of the United Kingdom, but can only be used for military, not commercial or any other purposes. They are the only parts of the UK where just the euro, not the pound, is in circulation – a scenario that remains unchanged even after Britain's departure from the EU.

Akrotiri and Dhekelia have their own legal system, distinct from the UK and Cyprus, but kept as close as possible to the laws of the latter.

The Court of the Sovereign Base Area is concerned with non-military offences, committed by any person within Akrotiri and Dhekelia. Law and order is maintained by the Sovereign Base Areas Police, while military law is upheld by the Cyprus Joint Police Unit.

There is no specific citizenship available for the bases.

Because they are run as military units, the Sovereign Base Area Administration reports to the British Ministry of Defence in London, rather than the Foreign and Commonwealth Office.

They are a British Overseas Territory, with a civilian administration working under an Administrator who is Commander of the British Forces, Cyprus.

Dhekelia (81 sq km) also has four enclaves within its territory; they are all exclaves of the Republic of Cyprus, sovereign territory of the Greek Cypriot government. They include the fully-enveloped villages of Ormideia and Xylotymvou and Dhekelia Power Station along the coast, which is cut in two by a British road. The enclaves appeared in 1960 as the UK tried to avoid including villages, cities and agricultural areas in its military bases.

Part of Dhekelia is also the area of Ayios Nikolaos, linked to Dhekelia by a corridor which doubles as a UN buffer zone, with the Turkish area north of this line.

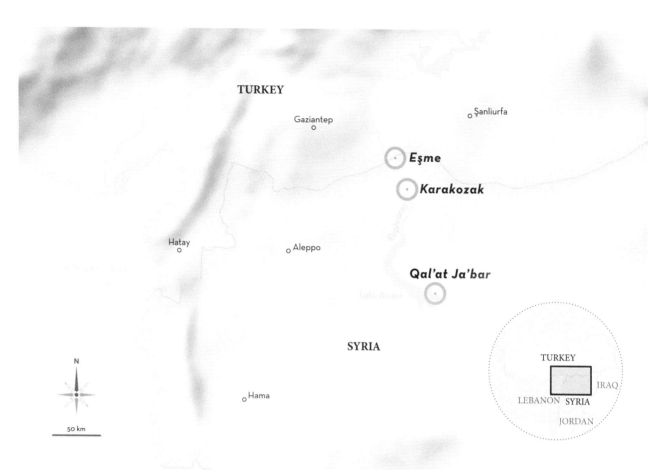

The Tomb of Suleyman Shah · Turkey/Syria

The world's only Turkish enclave, which changed location three times

The Tomb of Suleyman Shah is, according to Ottoman tradition, the grave that houses the relics of Suleyman Shah (c. 1178–1236), grandfather of Osman I (d. 1323/4), the founder of the Ottoman Empire. He is believed to have drowned in the Euphrates river in 1236 and was buried in what is now Syria. Since then, this legendary tomb has had three locations, all in present-day Syria.

From 1236 until 1973, it was near castle Qal'at Ja'bar in present-day Raqqa Governorate, Syria, where Suleyman Shah supposedly drowned.

Since the Treaty of Lausanne (1923) that broke up the Ottoman Empire into Turkey, Syria, and other states, the tomb site is officially the property of Turkey, making it the world's only Turkish enclave.

In 1973, the construction of the Tabqa Dam threatened to flood the tomb's location under the newly created Lake Assad, but Turkey and Syria agreed to move the tomb 85 km north to the Euphrates river in Syria, 27 km from the Turkish border.

On 21 February 2015, during the Syrian Civil War, Islamic militants threatened to attack the tomb site unless Turkish troops guarding it were withdrawn within three days. The tomb was unilaterally moved again by Turkey to a new site in Syria, just 180 metres from the Turkish border, 22 km west of Kobanî, during the so-called Operation Shah Euphrates. A convoy of 572 Turkish troops, 39 tanks and 57 armoured vehicles evacuated the 38 Turkish soldiers guarding the tomb. The rest of the old mausoleum was demolished.

The Turkish government stated the relocation, which is officially temporary, does not constitute any change to the status of the tomb site. The Syrian government said the raid was an act of "flagrant aggression" and broke the original agreement of 1923, holding Ankara accountable for any repercussions. In 2018, Turkey's Deputy Prime Minister, Fikri Işık, said the tomb would be relocated to its original location in northern Syria.

Novorossiysk

RUSSIA

Pyatigorsk

Sochi

▲ 5 642 m

Groznyy

Sukhumi

▲ 5 203 m

North
Ossetia

Vladikavkaz

Caucasus

Abkhazia

▲ 5 047 m

Mountains

South Ossetia

Tskhinvali

Poti

Gori

Tbilisi

Batumi

GEORGIA

N

Artvin

TURKEY

ARMENIA

AZERBAIJAN

200 km

Yerevan

Abkhazia

An independent 'state' internationally recognised only by Russia, Syria, Nauru,
Vanuatu, Nicaragua and Venezuela – and a holiday hotspot for Russians

Situated in the north-west corner of Georgia, with the Black Sea to the south-west and the Caucasus mountains and Russia to the north-east, Abkhazia (area 8,660 sq km, population 245,246) was once known as a prime holiday destination for the Soviet elite.

The region won a war of secession with Georgia from 1992–93, and formally declared independence in 1999.

After the war between Georgia and Russia from 1992–1993, and despite having most of its infrastructure destroyed, Abkhazia managed to redevelop its main economic pillars of tourism and agriculture. Although many efforts were made to rebuild after the war, the region was still occupied by Russia, with much of the territory destroyed. The ongoing conflict between Georgia and Russia slowed development.

In August 2008, fighting resumed during the South Ossetia War (see page 109), followed by the formal recognition of Abkhazia by Russia, the annulment of the 1994 ceasefire agreement and termination of missions by the United Nations and Commonwealth of Independent States.

After the Georgian–Russian war in 2008, Moscow recognised the region as an independent state. Georgia responded by declaring Abkhazia "occupied" by Russia.

In recent years, Abkhazia has drifted closer to Russia. In 2009 Moscow signed a five-year agreement with Abkhazia to take formal control of its frontiers with Georgia proper.

In 2014, Russia and the breakaway region signed a "strategic partnership", angering Georgia, which accused Moscow of seeking to annex Abkhazia.

Abkhazia's status as an independent state is internationally recognised only by Russia, Nauru, Nicaragua, Vanuatu and Venezuela.

The country depends on Russian support and currency, and has an uncertain political situation similar to that of South Ossetia (see page 109). From a travel perspective, it is entirely an independent territory.

Abkhazia has two official languages: Abkhaz and Russian. Abkhaz belongs to the north-west Caucasian linguistic family and is related to the Abkhaz–Adyghe language group in the same family. Russian is convenient for inter-cultural communication since Abkhazia is a multi-ethnic state.

Despite the country's controversial status, it remains a popular place to spend summer vacations among Russians.

Novorossiysk

RUSSIA

Pyatigorsk

Sochi

Abkhazia

Groznyy

5 642 m

Sukhumi

C a u c a s u s

5 203 m

North
Ossetia

Vladikavkaz

5 047 m

**South
Ossetia**

Tskhinvali

M o u n t a i n s

Poti

Gori

Batumi

GEORGIA

Tbilisi

N

Artvin

TURKEY

ARMENIA

AZERBAIJAN

200 km

Yerevan

South Ossetia

A state recognised as independent only
by Russia, Venezuela, Nicaragua, Nauru, Syria – but not by the UN

South Ossetia, officially the Republic of South Ossetia, or formerly the Tskhinvali Region of Georgia, is a mini-state recognised as independent only by Russia, Venezuela, Nicaragua, Nauru and Syria. It has a population of 53,000 people who live in an area of 3,900 sq km, with 30,000 in the capital, Tskhinvali.

While Georgia lost control of South Ossetia in the war of the early 1990s supported by Russia, the Georgian government and most members of the UN consider the territory part of Georgia.

South Ossetia is separated from Russia's North Ossetia region by a border running high in the Caucasus Mountains. Much of the region lies more than 1,000 metres above sea level. The country is inhabited mostly by Ossetians, who speak a language distantly related to Persian. Most ethnic Georgians have been displaced from the region by the two conflicts. As the Russian empire expanded into the area in the eighteenth and nineteenth centuries, the Ossetians did not join other peoples of the North Caucasus in putting up fierce resistance. They sided with the Bolshevik forces that occupied Georgia in the early 1920s and, as part of the carve-up which followed, the South Ossetian Autonomous Region was created in Georgia, and North Ossetia in Russia.

In the twilight years of the Soviet Union, when nationalist leader Zviad Gamsakhurdia came to power in Georgia, separatist sentiment burgeoned in South Ossetia. After several outbreaks of violence, the region declared its intention to secede from Georgia in 1990, and in 1992 proclaimed independence.

Sporadic violence involving Georgian irregular forces and Ossetian fighters continued until the summer of 1992, when agreement on the deployment of Georgian, Ossetian and Russian peacekeepers was reached.

Tensions came to a head again in August 2008 when, after nearly a week of clashes between Georgian troops and separatist forces, Georgia launched a concerted air and ground assault attack on Tskhinvali. Within days, Russian forces swept the Georgians out of South Ossetia and Abkhazia (see page 107), briefly pursuing them into Georgia proper.

Russia formally recognised South Ossetia (and Abkhazia) as an independent state after the war. In April 2009, Russia bolstered its position in South Ossetia by signing a five-year agreement to take formal control of its frontiers with Georgia proper (and those of Abkhazia).

In 2015, Russia started to put more pressure on Georgia over South Ossetia, and signed an "alliance and integration agreement" with South Ossetia that abolished border checkpoints. Georgia viewed this as a step towards Russian annexation of the region and expressed further concern when Russian forces pushed the border fence 1.5 km further into Georgia proper – a short distance from the country's main west–east highway.

Today, it is not possible to visit South Ossetia from Georgia. The only way is via Vladikavkaz in Russia.

RUSSIA

Tbilisi

GEORGIA

Ashagi Askipara
Yaradullu

AZERBAIJAN

ARMENIA

Nagorno-Karabakh

Yerevan

Stepanakert

Mount Ararat
5 137 m ▲

TURKEY

Nakhitchevan

Kapan

Meghri

IRAN

Tabriz

N

100 km

Nagorno Karabakh · Armenia/Azerbaijan

Europe's most fought-for enclave

Back in the news since 2021 amid the war between Armenia and Azerbaijan, Nagorno-Karabakh is an administrative territorial entity in the Transcaucasus between the two warring countries. It is a self-proclaimed republic not recognised by any UN member state. The only formal recognition of Nagorno-Karabakh independence comes from three other self-proclaimed countries – Abkhazia (page 107), South Ossetia (page 109), and Transnistria (page 39).

Before 2021, Nagorno-Karabakh was part of Armenia, although Armenia never recognised it. Since 2021, it has become an exclave of Armenia within Azerbaijan (although Armenia continues to ignore it).

With 4,400 sq km, Nagorno-Karabakh (capital Stepanakert) has a population of 150,000, with about 80 per cent of them Armenians.

Since 1921, the region has been part of the Azerbaijan Soviet Socialist Republic as an administrative territorial unit, with the rights of broad autonomy. In 1923, it received the status of an Autonomous region (NKAO) within the Azerbaijan SSR.

In 1987, 75,000 signatures backing reunification with Armenia were collected from Nagorno-Karabakh citizens and sent to the Central Committee of the Communist Party of the Soviet Union. It provoked a negative reaction from Azerbaijani authorities. The next year the regional council of the NKAO asked the Supreme Soviet to consider transferring the region to Armenia, but this request was seen as a manifestation of nationalism. In four months, the regional council made one more attempt and declared its secession from Azerbaijan. In response, the Presidium of the USSR Supreme Soviet adopted a resolution denying the possibility of transfer.

After the attempts at peaceful transition failed in September 1988, armed clashes began between Armenians and Azerbaijanis, which turned into a protracted conflict.

On 2 September 1991, the region was proclaimed to be the Nagorno-Karabakh Republic (NKR) as part of the USSR – less than four months before the latter's collapse. It included the territories of the NKAO, Shaumyan district and part of the Khanlar district of Azerbaijan.

This marked the beginning of open, armed confrontation between Armenia and Azerbaijan for control of the region from 1991–1994. The Karabakh conflict was the first major armed confrontation on the territory of the former Soviet Union. After the collapse of the USSR on 31 December 1991, Soviet internal troops were withdrawn and the conflict zone spiralled out of control.

The fighting escalated in May 1992, when the self-defence units of Karabakh took control over the city of Shusha, from which Azerbaijani troops regularly bombarded Stepanakert and surrounding villages.

In 1994, the NKR defence forces established control over 90 per cent of the former NKAO territory and also occupied fully or partially seven border regions of Azerbaijan, making up 8 per cent of the country. In turn, Azerbaijan retained control over parts of the Martuni, Martakert and Shahumyan districts of the NKR.

On 5 May 1994, a ceasefire agreement, known as the Bishkek Protocol, was signed by the parties with the mediation of Russia and Kyrgyzstan. Since then, the parties have repeatedly accused each other of violating the ceasefire, with numerous firearms incidents on the border.

The situation in the Nagorno-Karabakh conflict zone escalated sharply in 2014, 2016 (the so-called "four-day war") and particularly in the summer of 2021, when both Armenia and Azerbaijan declared a state of war. On 10 November 2021, Armenia, Azerbaijan and Russia signed an agreement ending hostilities, but the ceasefire has been breached repeatedly.

RUSSIA

Tbilisi

GEORGIA

Yukhari

Ashagi Askipara

Barkhudarli

Yaradullu

Kura

Artsvashen

AZERBAIJAN

ARMENIA

Yerevan

Nagorno-Karabakh

Karki

Stepanakert

Mount Ararat
5 137 m ▲

TURKEY

Nakhitchevan

Kapan

Nakhitchevan

Meghri

IRAN

Tabriz

N

100 km

Nakhitchevan · Armenia/Azerbaijan

After Nagorno-Karabakh, the other large exclave
between Armenia and Azerbaijan

Nakhitchevan is a region of the Caucasus and an autonomous republic of Azerbaijan. Although this region has borders with Iran, Armenia and Turkey, it remains very isolated, as it is not geographically linked to the rest of Azerbaijan, effectively making it an exclave of the country.

Nakhitchevan has a population of around 400,000, who are mostly of Turkish origin, Muslim Shiites (as is the case in Azerbaijan) and Azerbaijani speakers. The Armenian population in the region was forced to flee in the 1990s in the aftermath of the war between Armenia and Azerbaijan. Nakhitchevan not being dragged into the war between its two neighbours is partly thanks to the 1921 Treaty of Moscow, which designated Turkey as a guarantor despite its obvious geopolitical interests in supporting Azerbaijan. Azerbaijani originates from the Altaic family of languages, as do Turkish, Turkmen, Crimean Tatar or Gagauz (to the south of Moldova).

After a succession of wars and power struggles between historic Armenia and the Persian and Ottoman empires, the region was annexed by Russia in 1828. When western Armenia integrated into the Soviet Union in 1921, Stalin decreed that the region would become autonomous and part of Azerbaijan.

Nakhitchevan, with less than 50 per cent of the population comprised of Armenians before its Sovietisation, was to subsequently lose almost its whole Armenian population to emigration and a pro-Azerbaijani policy in the exclave during the Soviet era.

In 1926, Armenians constituted an estimated 15 per cent of the population of Nakhitchevan. Since the 1980s, their number has not risen above two per cent.

Nakhitchevan joined Azerbaijan in 1991 when the latter was formed, after the dissolution of the USSR.

A former cultural treasure of Armenia, the cemetery of Djoulfa once hosted the largest collection of khatchkars (tombstones) in historic Armenia, totalling about 13,000 shortly before its destruction, many from the end of the sixteenth and the beginning of the seventeenth centuries. It was demolished between 1998 and 2005 and a military base built in its place. The 89 Armenian churches in Nakhitchevan suffered the same fate in the 1990s.

Since the end of the last war between Armenia and Azerbaijan in 2020, Azerbaijan has been trying to negotiate the creation of a corridor— the Zangezur, or Meghri corridor—along Armenia's southern border which would link Nakhitchevan to the rest of Azerbaijan. Armenia, though, is reluctant, and Russia has numerous interests in the area and fears a renewal of Pan-Turkish feeling (the corridor would provide a direct link between Istanbul and Baku). For the moment, among other reasons, these have prevented the corridor from being created. Azerbaijan has begun talks to set up another corridor, running through Iran, linking Nakhitchevan with the rest of Azerbaijan.

Other enclaves between Armenia and Azerbaijan:

There are other, considerably smaller, exclaves between Armenia and Azerbaijan, to the north of these two countries and Nagorno-Karabakh.

- Artsvashen is an Armenian enclave in Azerbaijan, 2 km from its border. It has been governed by Azerbaijan since the Nagorno-Karabakh war in 1992.
- To the far north-east of Armenia are three small Azerbaijani exclaves in the heart of Armenian territory. Barkhudarli, Yukhari Askipara and Ashagi Askipara have been governed by Armenia since 1989.
- Around 5 km to the north of Nakhitchevan, Karki is an Azerbaijani village enclaved in Armenia. It has been controlled by the Armenian military since 1989.
- Lastly, even if it cannot strictly be referred to as an exclave, Yaradullu is an Azerbaijani village on the northern border between Armenia and Azerbaijan which is governed by Armenia.

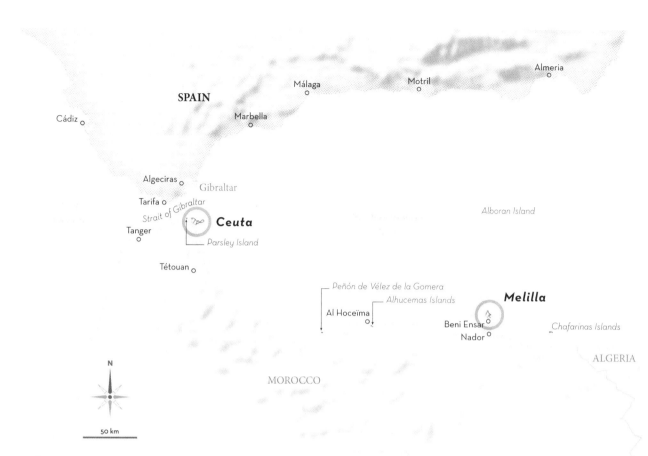

SPAIN

Cádiz

Málaga

Marbella

Motril

Almería

Algeciras

Gibraltar

Tarifa

Strait of Gibraltar

Ceuta

Tanger

Parsley Island

Tétouan

Alboran Island

Peñón de Vélez de la Gomera

Alhucemas Islands

Melilla

Al Hoceïma

Beni Ensar

Chafarinas Islands

Nador

ALGERIA

N

MOROCCO

50 km

Templū Summū

S. Iacobi

Castrum

S. Catarina

Per hanc portam ingressi
sunt primum Lusitani in
hoc oppidum

The Spanish possessions on the Moroccan coast · Spain/Morocco

Spanish exclaves in Africa

Ceuta and Melilla are relatively well known but there are five, not two, Spanish possessions on Morocco's Mediterranean shores (even if some geographers do not consider them as enclaved, as they have access to the sea). Along with Ceuta and Melilla, there are also the Chafarinas Islands, the Alhucemas Islands and the Vélez de la Gomera Rock. Parsley Island, the scene of a military incident between Spain and Morocco in 2002, is inhabited and is claimed by Spain to belong to Ceuta.

Ceuta (population 80,000) and its sister city Melilla (population 86,000), situated 400 km south-east along the coast, trace their Spanish past to the fifteenth century.

Coveted by Morocco, they have long been a flashpoint in diplomatic relations with Spain. Madrid asserts that both territories are integral parts of Spain and have the same status as the semi-autonomous regions on its mainland, such as the Basque and Catalan regions.

For centuries, Ceuta and Melilla were vital port cities protecting Spanish ships and acting as trading posts between Europe and Africa. Due to its geography, Spain has always had a close relationship with Africa. Phoenicians based in Carthage in what is today Tunisia established settlements on the Spanish coast.

Ceuta came under European control on 21 August 1415, when King John I of Portugal launched a surprise invasion of the city. It served as a trading outpost for goods that came from inland Africa and as a base to control much of northern Morocco.

From 1580 to 1640, Spain and Portugal were united during the Iberian Union, when the city attracted more people from Spain than Portugal due to proximity. When Portugal regained independence in 1640, Ceuta was the only part of the country with loyalties to Spain. In 1668, Portugal ceded the territory to Spain in the Treaty of Lisbon. In 1694, the Moroccans laid an unsuccessful siege to Ceuta until 1720, and again from 1721 to 1727.

Melilla came under Spanish control in 1497 after the city had been all but abandoned by Islamic rulers. As with Ceuta, the Moroccans made attempts at taking the city, but it was never a high priority. Given its proximity to Algeria, Melilla had a small trade war with France, which controlled Algeria in the early twentieth century.

In the 1930s, Spanish troops garrisoned in the two cities played a major role in future dictator Francisco Franco's uprising against their government.

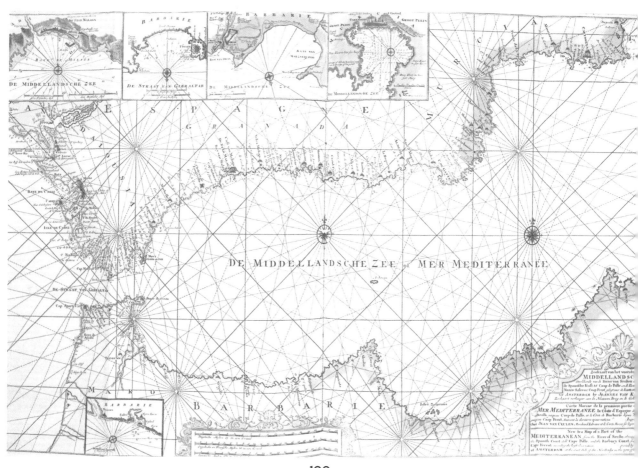

When Morocco gained independence from France in 1956, after more than four decades of rule by Spain and France, Spain refused to include Ceuta and Melilla in the handover. Morocco has made numerous claims to the territories since gaining independence.

In 2002, the dispute turned violent after a small group of Moroccan soldiers set up camp on the Spanish-controlled Parsley Island, 200 metres off the coast of mainland Morocco. They were forcefully removed by the Spanish navy in a clash that heightened tensions between the two countries.

Spanish King Juan Carlos angered Moroccans by visiting Melilla in 2007 and Morocco's King Mohammed VI briefly recalled his ambassador to Madrid in protest over the Spanish king's visit to "occupied territories".

Razor wire fences surround both enclaves. They were first introduced in 2005, but were removed two years later after an outcry over the wounds sustained by people trying to climb them. In 2013, Spanish PM Mariano Rajoy reintroduced the wire after waves of migrants tried to breach the country's border. The move was branded inhumane by political opponents, activists and senior Catholic bishops.

Unemployment in the native workforce is more than 30 per cent, among the highest rates in Spain. The cities are a magnet for thousands of traders and menial workers who cross from Morocco each day.

Peñón de Vélez de la Gomera (in English, Vélez de la Gomera Rock), known to the Moroccans as Rocher de Badis (or simply Badis), is a peninsula 260 km west of Melilla and 117 km south-west of Ceuta. It has been a Spanish possession since 1564.

The Zafarin Islands (otherwise known as the Chafarinas Islands) have 200 inhabitants and are a group of three small islands 3.3 km from the Moroccan village Ras El Ma (Cap de l'Eau) and 46 km south-east of Melilla. They have been under Spanish control since 1848.

The Alhucemas Islands are another archipelago of three small islands under Spanish control, 155 km east of Ceuta, 100 km from Melilla and 4 km north-east of the Moroccan town of Al Hoceïma. The Peñón de Alhucemas is situated 800 metres from the coast and the other islands – Isla de Mar and Isla de Tierra – are only 50 metres off the Moroccan coasts. The Peñón de Alhucemas has a barracks with 350 soldiers. The two other islands are uninhabited.

Parsley Island (Isla de Perejil in Spanish) is a small island between Spain and Morocco, 250 metres from the Moroccan coasts and 8 km from the Spanish town of Ceuta, 13.5 km from the Spanish mainland. To Spain, in administrative terms, it is part of Ceuta.

Further away from the coasts, Alborán, also known as the 'navel of the sea' to the Arabs, is a Spanish Mediterranean island 57 km north of Melilla. The island has belonged to Spain since 1540, but that is disputed by Morocco.

© Ignacio Gavira

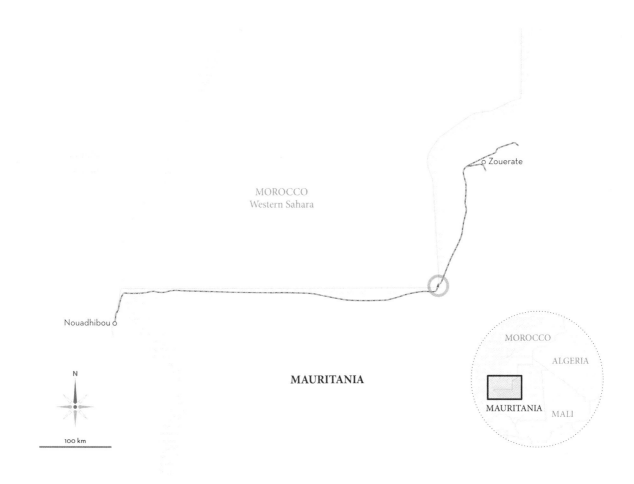

MOROCCO
Western Sahara

o Zouerate

Nouadhibou o

N

MAURITANIA

100 km

MOROCCO

ALGERIA

MAURITANIA

MALI

122

The desert train · Mauritania

A rare train that runs through another country for 5 km,
allowing entry to Western Sahara without a visa

Built between 1961 and 1963, Mauritania's only railway line runs for 704 km, linking the iron mine of Zouérat in the north of the country to the port of Nouadhibou on the Atlantic coast.

Constructed in the colonial period by France (Mauritania was part of French West Africa), the special feature of the line is a large detour along the former colony's border with the erstwhile Spanish colony of Rio de Oro (today known as Western Sahara, a territory that was disputed between Morocco and the Polisario Front), without entering what was Spanish territory. This is how, in difficult and mountainous terrain, the 2 km-long tunnel of Choum was built, 460 km from Nouadhibou, where the border between the two countries forms a right angle.

Since 1991 and until the end of the Western Sahara Conflict (even if the conflict between Morocco and the Polisario Front is far from over), a 5 km-long track has been built across Western Sahara on much flatter territory than that of the tunnel, avoiding a difficult climb for trains often heavily loaded with iron ore. The train is, in fact, considered one of the longest (and heaviest) in the world: it is pulled by three or four locomotives and can reach a length of 2.5 km with up to 210 wagons. Occasionally, carriages for passengers are added to the goods wagons.

LEBANON

SYRIA

IRAQ

West
Bank

Gaza

Damietta
Port Said

Alexandria

ISRAEL

JORDAN

Cairo   Suez

SAUDI ARABIA

Asyut

EGYPT

Luxor

Aswan

Lake Nasser

L y b i a n   D e s e r t

Wadi Halfa Salient

Wadi Halfa

N u b i a n   D e s e r t

Port Sudan

Dongola

Merowe

SUDAN

ERYTHREA

Khartoum

N

500 km

Wadi Halfa Salient · Egypt/Sudan

A unique, condominium-like border protrusion,
currently controlled by Egypt

The border of Egypt and Sudan is a long straight line for almost its whole length. Almost, because in the eastern part there are two disruptions on this line: one east in an area called Bir Tawil (see page 127), and one on the Nile, called Wadi Halfa.

The Wadi Halfa Salient, named after a nearby Sudanese city 22 km south of the border, is a salient of the international border between Egypt and the Sudan along the Nile river to the north.

On 19 January 1899, the United Kingdom and Egypt (which had occupied Sudan since the nineteenth century, but had been under British occupation since 1882) defined the southern border of 'Sudan' as the territories south of the 22nd parallel, hence the artificial straight line of today's border.

Two months later, on 26 March 1899, the border was changed in the Wadi Halfa area in favour of Sudan, to give the country a northern terminal at the city of Faras for a planned railway line from Khartoum. Also, access to the area north of the border along the Nile was easier from the Sudan. In 1902 a new administrative border was established, deviating north of the 22nd parallel north along the Nile and placing the area under Sudanese administration.

The Wadi Halfa Salient is finger-shaped, roughly 9 kilometres wide and is on both sides of the original course of the Nile, 25 kilometres to the north into Egyptian territory, with a total area of 210 sq km.

Most of the area was flooded by the completion of the Aswan Dam in July 1970 and the creation of the 550 km-long and 35 km-wide Lake Nasser reservoir. This affected most villages of the area and the ancient city of Faras. Some people were resettled to New Halfa in the Butana region.

Before the flooding, more than 50 villages could be found in the area, of which 24 were west and 29 east of the Nile, along with one unnamed village on Faras Island in the river. The largest town, and the only one with a population exceeding 2,000, was Dubayrah.

The Bir Tawil (see page 127) is still disputed. Egypt now claims the original border of 1899 along the 22nd degree north, while Sudan wants the amended border of 1902, i.e. the same areas as Egypt.

While there have been disputes about the Hala'ib Triangle and military occupation by Egypt, the area of the Wadi Halfa Salient remained relatively obscure, because most of the area had been flooded by Lake Nasser. The area is currently controlled by Egypt.

LEBANON

SYRIA

IRAQ

West
Bank

Damietta

Gaza

Alexandria ○   ○   ○ Port Said

ISRAEL

JORDAN

○ Cairo   ○ Suez

SAUDI ARABIA

Asyut ○

EGYPT

○ Luxor

○ Aswan

Lake Nasser

Lybian Desert

Bir Tawil   *Hala'ib Triangle*

○ Wadi Halfa

Nubian Desert

○ Port Sudan

Dongola ○

○ Merowe

SUDAN

ERYTHREA

Khartoum ○

N

500 km

Bir Tawil · Egypt/Sudan

A truly unclaimed piece of land in the world

If you take a close look at the border of Egypt and Sudan, you will see an almost perfect, long, straight line. Almost, because in the eastern part there are two small disruptions in the line: one on the Nile (see Wadi Haifa page 125) and one east of the Nile, in an area called Bir Tawil (2,000 sq km).

On 19 January 1899, the UK and Egypt (which occupied Sudan from the nineteenth century, but had itself been under British occupation since 1882) defined the southern border of 'Sudan' as the territories south of the 22nd parallel of latitude, producing the imaginary straight line of today's border.

On 4 November 1902, however, because Bir Tawil was used as grazing land by the Ababda tribe, based near Aswan (Egypt), it was placed under the Egyptian administration. Similarly, the Hala'ib Triangle to the north-east of Bir Tawil, whose inhabitants were culturally closer to Khartoum (Sudan), was placed under the British governor of Sudan.

Having achieved independence in December 1955, Sudan claimed official ownership of the Hala'ib Triangle, a much more valuable piece of land than the Bir Tawil area, which is only a tenth the size and has no permanent settlements, roads or access to the sea.

Acknowledging the difference in the importance of both lands, however, Egypt disputed the claim, stating that the 1902 administrative boundary was temporary. As such, from the Egyptian point of view, the Hala'ib Triangle belonged to Egypt, and the Bir Tawil was Sudan's.

Egypt and Sudan have never resolved their boundary dispute: neither wants to claim ownership of Bir Tawil which, they both believe, would imply they have to relinquish ownership of the Hala'ib Triangle. As a result, both states claim Hala'ib and neither claims the much less valuable Bir Tawil. With no third state claiming that neglected area, Bir Tawil remains one of the few land patches of the world not claimed by any internationally recognised state.

Jeremiah Heaton, a US farmer with a messianic bent, tried to take possession of Bir Tawil in 2014. He travelled there and, after setting up a flag on the land, began a campaign to develop his new 'state'. But, instead of receiving praise for his actions, he was publicly labelled "a twenty-first-century imperialist" and had to give up his claim.

Likoma and Chizumulu islands · Malawi/Mozambique

Two Malawi islands entirely surrounded by Mozambican territorial waters and a disputed lake border

Lake Malawi is a huge landlocked body of water (29,000 sq km) that belongs to Malawi and Mozambique, and draws the border between Malawi and Tanzania. Surprisingly, the border between Malawi and Tanzania is not in the middle of the lake, but on the Tanzanian shore, as agreed in the 1890 Anglo–German Treaty (the British colonial government, just after capturing Tanganyika from Germany, unilaterally placed all the waters of the lake under the single jurisdiction of their former Nyasaland colony). The agreement is backed, according to Malawi, by the 1964 Cairo Resolution that froze African territories along the borders inherited from colonial powers at independence, to cement African unity. Tanzania disagrees and relies on the tradition within international law that a median position on the lake is the boundary, giving both states large parts of the lake.

Originally named Lake Nyasa by David Livingstone in 1859, after 'Nyasaland' (the British Protectorate name for Malawi before the country gained independence in 1964), the lake covers an entire third of the country from top to bottom, and forms a natural boundary between Malawi and Tanzania and Malawi and Mozambique.

The lake's uniqueness lies in the fact that, just a few kilometres from Mozambique, its two islands (Likoma and Chizumulu) both belong to Malawi, although they are surrounded by Mozambican territorial waters, which makes them de facto exclaves of Malawi. If you take a boat from anywhere in Malawi to Likoma or Chizumulu, you have to go through Mozambique. The reason is the islands were colonised by Anglican missionaries from Nyasaland, rather than by the Portuguese who colonised Mozambique. In response to a plea by David Livingstone in 1880, missionaries from the Universities' Mission to Central Africa established their headquarters on Likoma Island. The British originally claimed the whole of Lake Nyasa/Lake Malawi (like they did with Germany for today's Tanzania/Malawi border, see above), but in 1954 signed an agreement with Portugal which recognised the centre of the lake as the boundary between their colony and Mozambique.

The lake is the second deepest in Africa, the fourth largest freshwater lake in the world by volume, and home to the most species of fish. Lake Malawi has a greater diversity of fish species than the whole of Europe and North America combined.

British Empire's first naval victory of World War I

One interesting historical fact about Lake Malawi is that it saw some action during World War I. When the war was declared, Captain Rhoades, of the *SS Gwendolen* on Lake Nyasa, was ordered to "sink, burn and destroy" the *Hermann Von Wissmann*, the only German Empire boat on the lake. It was sunk by a single cannon shell fired from the *SS Gwendolen*. The battle became known as the British Empire's first naval victory of World War I.

Caprivi Strip · Namibia

Created for access to the Zambezi River,
the geographical oddity finally proved unnavigable …

The Caprivi Strip is a 450 km-long, 30 km-wide corridor protruding from the north-east corner of Namibia. It feels as far removed from the rest of the country as it looks on the map. It is bordered by Angola and Zambia to the north and Botswana to the south.

The Caprivi Strip was named after Leo von Caprivi, who was the Chancellor of the German Empire between 1890 and 1894, succeeding the more famous Otto von Bismarck.

In July 1890, in the so-called Heligoland–Zanzibar treaty (already in preparation during Bismarck times), he ceded to the British Empire Zanzibar (1,666 sq km) and Swahililand (3,000 sq km) in exchange for the small island of Heligoland (1.7 sq km), a few kilometres off the coast of north-west Germany, which helped secure this border.

The treaty also gave Germany the Caprivi Strip, which was added to the existing German South West Africa (today's Namibia), but recognised the British Empire's ownership of Ngamiland, a small piece of land in north-west Bechuanaland (today's Botswana), bordering the Caprivi Strip.

The idea was to link German South West Africa to the Zambezi River (at the eastern tip of the Caprivi Strip) and to the rest of Austral Africa and the Indian Ocean. In colonial times, control of navigable rivers was essential for commercial relations.

The river, however, proved to be not fully navigable because of the Victoria Falls further east.

Caprivi, as a part of Namibia, became independent on 21 March 1990.

AFRICA

Equator

Greenwich meridian

Recife ○

Ascension

Luanda ○

SOUTH
AMERICA

Saint Helena

Trindade and Martin Vaz

Rio de Janeiro
○

Tropic of Capricorn

Cape Town ○

*Cape
of Good Hope*

12° 18'

○
Montevideo

37° 7' ◯ **Tristan da Cunha**

Gough

Falkland

South Georgia

Bouvet

South Sandwich

South Shetlands

South Orkneys

Antarctic Circle

N

*Antarctica
Peninsula*

1 000 km

ANTARCTICA

Tristan da Cunha · Great Britain

The world's most remote human settlement

Tristan da Cunha (population 266) is a remote archipelago in the South Atlantic more than 2,000 km from the nearest human settlements of St Helena, and Cape Town in South Africa. It is the world's most remote human settlement.

The island group consists of Tristan da Cunha, Nightingale, Inaccessible, and Gough Islands. Gough and Inaccessible Islands are World Heritage Sites.After its discovery in 1506 by the Portuguese Tristan da Cunha, the first attempt to settle was made by Jonathon

Lambert, from Salem (Massachusetts, USA), who led a party of three men in 1810 to establish a trading station on Tristan, which he renamed "Reception" and wished to be known as the "Islands of Refreshment". Tomasso Corri from Livorno in Italy was the only survivor of this fledgling community when HMS Seiramis arrived in 1813. He reported that Lambert, with two companions, had drowned in a fishing accident. Legends of Tomasso's treasure are still current in the Tristan community and are explored in several books.

In the 1860s, Tristan da Cunha became increasingly isolated from shipping after three important world events. The 1861–1865 Civil War in the USA curtailed the already declining whaling industry, whose ships had often called on Tristan for supplies. The Suez Canal's opening in 1869 gave a safer and much quicker passage to Far East markets, avoiding the perils of the South Atlantic and Cape of Good Hope. Finally, steam replaced sail, effectively isolating Tristan da Cunha.

As World War II approached, German U-boats and the battleship Graf Spee were sighted off Tristan and, in 1942, a top secret naval station code named Job 9 (later HMS Atlantic Isle) was established on Tristan. Its role was to monitor U-boats, which in those days needed to surface to maintain radio contact, and maintain a meteorological station.

Tristan da Cunha was garrisoned by the British in 1816 to prevent any attempt to rescue Napoleon from St Helena.

AFRICA

Equator

Greenwich meridian

Recife ○

Ascension

Luanda ○

SOUTH
AMERICA

5° 42'

15° 58' ○ **Saint Helena**

Trindade and Martin Vaz

Rio de Janeiro ○

Tropic of Capricorn

○ Montevideo

Cape Town ○

Cape
of Good Hope

Tristan da Cunha

Gough

Falkland

South Georgia

Bouvet

South Sandwich

South Shetlands

South Orkneys

Antarctic Circle

N

Antarctica
Peninsula

ANTARCTICA

1 000 km

The French domains of Saint Helena ·
France/Great Britain

A French-owned property on an island belonging to the United Kingdom
due to Napoleon's exile there between 1815 and 1821

Saint Helena is a volcanic island spanning some 122 sq km located in the South Atlantic, 1,850 km west of the north-west coast of Namibia and the south-east coast of Brazil. Although the island is officially a British overseas territory belonging to the UK, it has buildings that officially belong to France.

The island is famous for being the place where Napoleon I went into exile from 14 October 1815 until his death on 5 May 1821. Historically, the island exerted an important strategic role over the passage of the East India Company's fleet, which it lost when the Suez Canal was opened in 1869.

Today, the French domains of Saint Helena cover 14 hectares, including Longwood House and the Valley of the Tomb in the district of Longwood, and Briars pavilion in the Alarm Forest district.

The domains are home to a museum, and exhibitions on the life of the emperor are held there. The French Ministry of Foreign Affairs ensures the upkeep of the buildings and land, which have been administratively attached to the French consulate in Cape Town, South Africa, since 2004.

Detained at Longwood House from 1815, Napoleon died there in 1821. The next day, the governor of the island, Sir Hudson Lowe, is quoted as saying to those around him: "Well, gentlemen, he was England's greatest enemy and mine too, but I forgive him for everything. On the death of such a great man, we must only feel deep pain and sorrow."

In accordance with his last wishes, Napoleon was buried, on 9 May, near a spring, in Geranium valley, which is now known as the Valley of the Tomb. On 27 May, the whole French colony left the island. In 1840, the king of France's request to reclaim the emperor's body was granted by the UK. Napoleon's body was sent back to France and buried in the Invalides, in Paris.

Napoleon III bought Longwood House and the Valley of the Tomb from the British government in 1858, and named it "The French domains of Saint Helena". Briars pavilion, the emperor's first home on the island, was added to the domain in 1959 when its last owner donated it to France.

Sainte-Hélène. — Habitation impériale de Long-Wood.

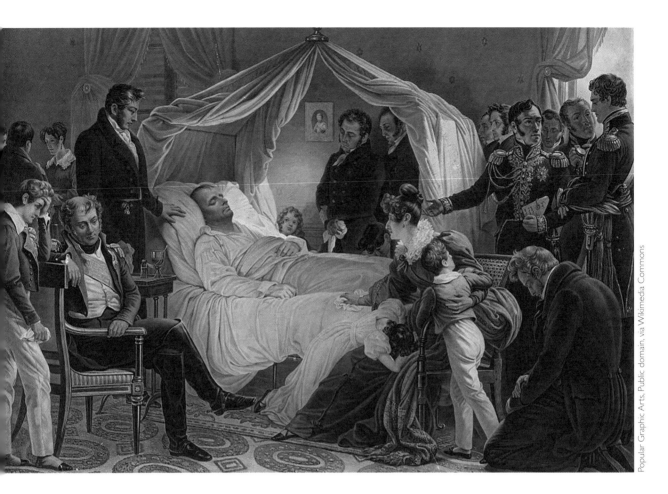

IRAN

Bandar Abbas

Strait of Hormuz

IRAN
PAKISTAN
SAUDI
ARABIA   UAE   OMAN

YEMEN

Ras al Khaimah

Sharjah

Nahwa → *Madha*

Dubai

Fujairah

N

UNITED
ARAB EMIRATES

OMAN

Abu Dhabi

100 km

Madha and Nahwa · Oman/UAE

An enclave of Oman within the UAE and an enclave of the UAE within the enclave of Oman …

United Arab Emirates (UAE) geography is confusing. This may be due to some territories in the region having been owned by different ruling families before the birth of the UAE; it was not unusual for the landowner families to exchange gifts of land and to change ruler allegiance.

With a population of around 3,000, Madha is an Omani exclave inside the UAE. It is bordered in the UAE by Sharjah (Khor Fakkan), Fujairah and Ras al Khaimah. Madha became part of Oman around 80 years ago, when its people chose to align themselves with the Omani Sultan rather than the leaders of Ras al Khaimah, Fujairah or Sharjah, as they believed Oman could help them more.

With an area of just 75 sq km, Nahwa is an enclave of the UAE within the Omani enclave of Madha. As such, it is one of the very few counter-enclaves of the world, along with the ones at Baarle, at the border between Belgium and the Netherlands (see page 57).

The origins of this situation date back to the 1930s, when Madha villagers invited the leaders of local clans to a feast. Each clan pledged loyalty to Oman, except Nahwa, which had closer ties with Sharjah (today's UAE) and chose to stay associated with that emirate.

The Musandam peninsula (1,800 sq km, 31,425 people) – see photo opposite –, part of Oman, is also an exclave, as it is separated from the rest of Oman by the UAE. Its location on the Strait of Hormuz gives Oman partial control, shared with Iran, of the strategic strait. The area became part of Oman after the British invaded the area in 1971 to bring it under the control of the Oman regime of Sultan Qaboos, who took power after a British-backed coup against his father.

KAZAKHSTAN

Almaty ○

Bishkek ○

Shymkent ○

UZBEKISTAN

Tashkent ○

KYRGYZSTAN

Bukhara ○   Samarkand ○

Kashgar ○

TAJIKISTAN

TURKMENISTAN

Dushanbe ○

CHINA

Mary ○

Bactria

Pamir

Wakhan Corridor

AFGHANISTAN

Kabul ○

Islamabad ○

PAKISTAN

New Delhi ○

IRAN

INDIA

N

500 km

Wakhan Corridor · Afghanistan

A narrow strip of territory in Afghanistan
designed to protect the British Empire from the Russian empire

The Wakhan Corridor is a narrow strip of territory in Afghanistan (350 km-long, but less than 14 km-wide) that lies between China, Tajikistan and Pakistan.

This strip of land was created in 1893 as a buffer zone between the territories of British India (including today's Pakistan and India) and Tsarist Russia (including today's Tajikistan).

The corridor is part of a political creation from The Great Game between the British Empire and Russian Empire for most of the nineteenth century and the beginning of the twentieth century. It was a fight for influence and power over Afghanistan and neighbouring territories in Central and South Asia.

In the north of the corridor, an agreement in 1873 made the Panj and Pamir Rivers the border between Afghanistan and the Russian Empire. In the south, the Durand Line was designed in 1893 by Mortimer Durand, a British diplomat of the Indian Civil Service, with Abdur Rahman Khan, the Afghan Emir.

This agreement, which marked the boundary between British India and Afghanistan, left a narrow strip of land ruled by Afghanistan as a buffer between the two empires, which became known as the Wakhan Corridor in the twentieth century.

The border with China, formally demarcated in 1963, is officially closed, making the Wakhan Corridor a particularly remote area.

The Wakhan Corridor has historically been an important transit path of the ancient Silk Road. Even Marco Polo used it. In the fourth and fifth centuries, the passes across the Pamir led Chinese pilgrims to the Buddhist centres in today's Afghanistan and India and were used by Persian merchants to sell their goods in the Chinese market. Until the collapse of the Mughal Empire in India, the Wakhan Corridor was one of the main routes for traders and merchants between India, China and major cities like Bactria and Bukhara in modern-day Afghanistan and Central Asia.

With the rapidly developing use of sea routes by Westerners to reach India and China in the late fifteenth century, the importance of the Wakhan Corridor and the Silk Road declined.

© Tom Hartley

© USAID U.S. Agency for International Development

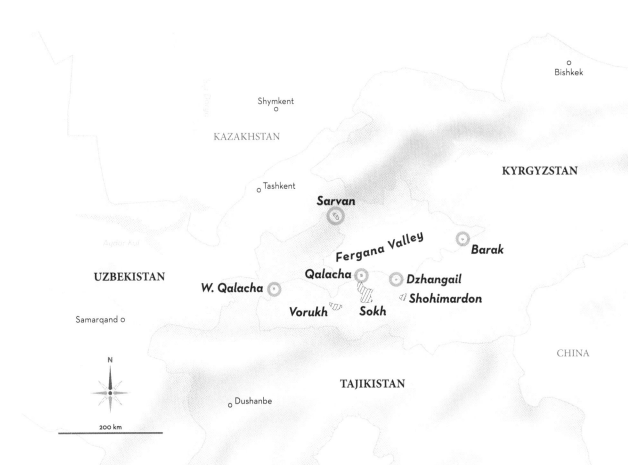

Enclaves of the Fergana Valley · Uzbekistan/Kyrgyzstan/ Tajikistan borders

The world's most disputed enclaves

Central Asia has one of the highest concentrations of enclaves and exclaves. The administrative borders in the Fergana Valley, shared between Kyrgyzstan, Tajikistan and Uzbekistan, were redrawn often during Soviet times, until the 1936 Constitution fixed most of the delimitations, at least on paper.

The total length of the Uzbek-Kyrgyz border is 1,379 km, with 1,055 km of them delimited, but the 28 sections in the Ala-Buka and Aksy districts, comprising a few enclaves established in the Soviet period and about 300 km of the border, are still disputed.

There are eight enclaves in the Fergana Valley, which is now divided between Kyrgyzstan, Uzbekistan, and Tajikistan. Uzbekistan has four exclaves in Kyrgyzstan, Tajikistan has three exclaves (one in Uzbekistan and two in Kyrgyzstan) and Kyrgyzstan has one tiny de facto exclave inside Uzbekistan.

The two largest Uzbek exclaves, Sokh and Shohimardon, are located in Kyrgyzstan. The biggest enclave, Sokh, consists of 19 villages and a 60,000 population (352 sq km) with 99 per cent of its population Tajiks. A local legend goes that a Kyrgyz communist party official lost it in a card game to his Uzbek opponent in 1955. Shohimardon (38.2 sq km, population 5,000, with 90 per cent Uzbeks and 10 per cent Kyrgyz) is a popular resort with several sanatoriums and is a place of pilgrimage. A folk legend claims the Caliph Ali is buried there, but almost everybody else believes he is buried in Najaf, Iraq.

Other Uzbek exclaves in Kyrgyzstan are tiny. Qalacha is 3.5 km long and 1 km at its widest, and Dzhangail (1.7 km long and 850 metres wide) is farmland and virtually uninhabited.

The area has four other enclaves: a tiny Tajik enclave inside Uzbekistan (Sarvan) and two Tajik enclaves inside Kyrgyzstan: Vorukh and Western Qalacha (Kaygarach). Kyrgyzstan also has one exclave inside Uzbekistan: Barak (4 sq km, population 627).

After deadly bombings in 1999 in the Uzbek capital, Tashkent, fears of Islamic terrorists entering the country led Uzbekistan to construct a barrier along much of its border with Kyrgyzstan in the fertile Ferghana Valley. Uzbekistan even laid land mines in the summer of 2000 along several parts of the border, with people and livestock accidentally killed and injured.

But while the comparatively easy disputes along the unmarked Uzbek-Kyrgyz border have been resolved, several areas of Uzbekistan surrounded by Kyrgyz territory remain disputed. The Uzbek citizens who live there must, in many cases, pass through Kyrgyz border posts to leave the exclaves. According to some experts, one option for officials in Tashkent and Bishkek to resolve the exclave issue involves Uzbekistan giving the territory within its two exclaves to Kyrgyzstan in exchange for a similar amount of Kyrgyz territory somewhere along the border. Such a trade would almost certainly include Barak.

Kyrgyzstan set a precedent in ceding territory when it agreed to give tens of thousands of acres in the Khan-Tengri mountains and the Uzbenku-Kuush Gorge to China in 1999 to resolve a border dispute with Beijing.

Some small bits of land have already been swapped by Uzbekistan and Kyrgyzstan under the deals signed by the countries' presidents in 2017 and 2018. But, before the 2021 conflict, Tajik President Emomali Rakhmon told his countrymen he had no plans for a land swap between the Vorukh exclave and Kyrgyz territory.

The origin of this complex border situation is not due to Stalin arbitrarily drawing the borders, as many people think, but to the collectivisation campaigns of the 1930s. The key was the collective farming, or not, of some areas which sometimes extended into neighbouring territories. An example of this was in 1975, when Kyrgyz people exchanged 1,000 hectares of land for 450 litres of water, creating almost immediate ethnic tension. As long as the Soviet Union existed, that was not such a problem, but when independence came after 1991, this became an international dispute.

Dahagram-Angarpota · India/Bangladesh

The last remaining enclave of Cooch Behar,
formerly the most complex border in the world

At its closest point, about 178 metres from the border of Bangladesh, Dahagram–Angarpota (17,000 people) is the only Bangladeshi enclave left in India. It is the last enclave of a complex patchwork of 198 enclaves and exclaves that made it the most complex border in the world. That was ended by an agreement between Bangladesh and India in 2015.

Cooch Behar was an independent principality until 1949, when it joined India after Indian independence (1947). It is now a district in the Indian state of West Bengal.

Until 2015, Cooch Behar possessed 106 exclaves in Bangladesh, totalling 70 sq km. Of those, three were counter-enclaves (enclaves within enclaves) and the world's only 'third-order', or counter-counter-enclave (enclave within enclave within enclave): Dahala Khagrabari (7,000 sq metres). The biggest Indian enclave was Balapara Khagrabari (26 sq km), the smallest Panisala (1,100 sq metres).

Conversely, Bangladesh possessed 92 exclaves inside India, comprising 50 sq km. Of these, 21 were counter-enclaves. The largest Bangladeshi exclave was Dahagram–Angarpota (18.7 sq km, and the only one that still exists) and the smallest was the counter-enclave of Upan Chowki Bhaini (53 sq metres), the smallest ever international enclave in the world.

An estimate for the total population of all the enclaves was 70,000, at the beginning of the twenty-first century.

The origins of most enclaves go back to 1713 when a treaty between the Mughal Empire and the Cooch Behar Kingdom reduced the latter's territory by one third. However, the Mughals did not manage to dislodge all Cooch Behar chieftains from the territory gained. At the same time, some Mughal soldiers retained lands within Cooch Behar proper while remaining loyal to the Mughal Empire. This territorial 'splintering' was not so remarkable in the context of that time: the subcontinent was extremely fragmented, similar to pre-1871 Germany. Most enclaves were economically self-sufficient and the fragmentation caused no significant border issues, as Cooch Behar was nominally tributary to the Mughals anyway.

In 1765, the British seized control of the Mughal territory by way of the East India Company, which in 1814 was surprised to discover extraterritorial dots of Cooch Behar within its territory. Those enclaves were sometimes used as sanctuary by offenders fleeing the police.

In 1947, the formerly Mughal territories became part of the eastern part of Pakistan (the western part being today's Pakistan) and Cooch Behar acceded to India only in 1949, as one of the last of the 600-odd, pre-independence Princely States to do so.

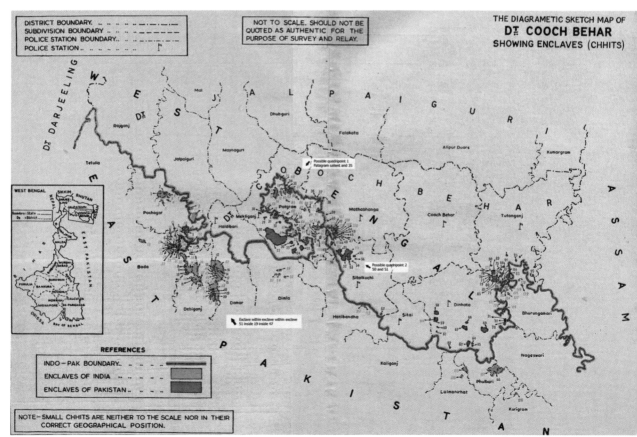

In 1971, East Pakistan gained independence as Bangladesh.

Remarkably, the enclave complex survived all these changes of sovereignty on both sides of the border – although the enclave complex used to be even more complicated before India's independence, with about 50 Cooch Behar exclaves in Assam and West Bengal rationalised away after all three entities became parts of India.

Attempts in 1958 and 1974 to exchange enclaves across the international border proved more elusive, even though the international aspect of these enclaves made administering them extremely unworkable, and thus such an exchange more useful than that of the all-Indian enclaves. The border situation has often made it impossible for people living in the enclaves to legally go to school, hospital or to market. Complicated agreements for policing and supplying the enclaves had to be drawn up: a 1950 list of products that could be imported into the enclaves included matches, cloth and mustard oil.

It all changed in September 2011, when India signed the Additional Protocol for the 1974 Land Boundary Agreement with Bangladesh, and both nations announced an intention to swap 162 enclaves, giving residents a choice of nationality.

Under the agreement, India received 51 of the 71 Bangladeshi enclaves that were inside India proper (28.7 sq km), while Bangladesh received 95 to 101 of the 103 Indian enclaves inside Bangladesh proper (69.4 sq km). According to the July 2010 joint census, there were 14,215 people residing in Bangladeshi enclaves in India and 37,269 people residing in Indian enclaves in Bangladesh. The people living in these enclaves without a citizenship were allowed to choose their nationality.

The agreement was finally ratified by both countries on 6 June 2015, and the former enclave residents took part in their first government elections in 2019.

© Amartya Bag at Flickr

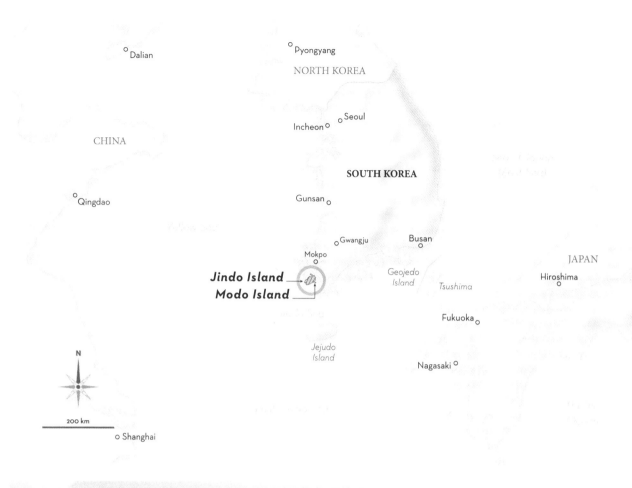

Dalian
Pyongyang
NORTH KOREA

Incheon ○ ○ Seoul

CHINA

SOUTH KOREA

Qingdao

Gunsan ○

Gwangju ○   Busan
Mokpo ○   JAPAN

Jindo Island   Geojedo   Hiroshima
Modo Island   Island   Tsushima

Fukuoka ○

Jejudo
Island

Nagasaki ○

N

200 km

○ Shanghai

Jindo Island · South Korea

Where, in one of the world's most amazing natural phenomena, the sea parts

The Jindo 'Moses Miracle' happens twice a year in Jindo island, the third largest in Korea, situated between Jejudo and Geojodo islands in the Jindo Sea, the northern portion of the East China Sea.

A few times each year (normally the end of February and mid-June), at low tide, a land path of 2.8 km long and 40 metres wide connecting the islands of Jindo and Modo is revealed for about an hour, before being submerged by the sea again.

During that hour, hundreds of people manage to walk across the sea between the islands.

This natural phenomenon resembles the parting of the Red Sea of biblical fame, hence the name.

At Jindo Island, the sea parting is no miracle, but the result of extremely low tides caused by tidal harmonics or, in plain speak, the gravity of the sun and moon pulling at the surface of the Earth. Each of these produces varying gravitational forces, resulting in several unique, recurrent, patterns in the tide.

At times, however, numerous tidal harmonics will line up to generate a very high or very low tide.

So, what could seem to be a biblical parting of the waters is, in reality, just a lowering of the entire sea level. As long as the shapes and locations of the islands remain unchanged, the sea parting will keep happening.

There is another, much more poetic, explanation of that phenomenon. According to a local legend, Jindo Island was once inhabited by tigers. When the creatures began threatening local villages, the people had no choice but to flee to Modo. One young woman, called Bbyong, was accidentally left behind. Desperate to be with her loved ones, she prayed day and night to Yongwang, the god of the ocean, until he finally told her in a dream that a rainbow would appear in the sea, so that she could cross it. She woke the next morning to find the sea had indeed parted, and a rainbow road led her to the island, where her family waited.

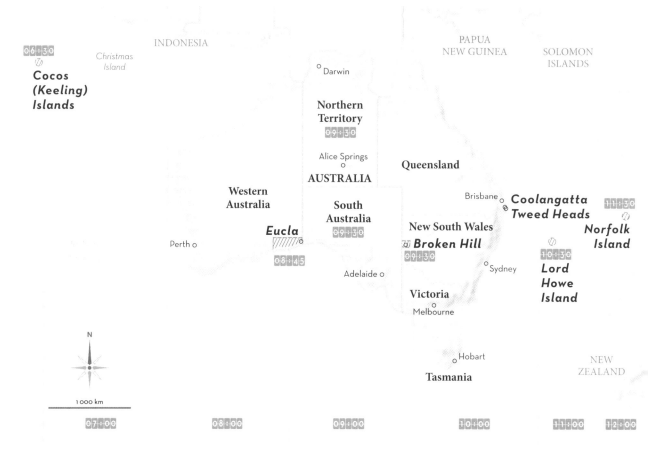

INDONESIA

PAPUA
NEW GUINEA

SOLOMON
ISLANDS

`06:30`

Christmas
Island

**Cocos
(Keeling)
Islands**

Darwin

**Northern
Territory**
`09:30`

Alice Springs

AUSTRALIA

**Western
Australia**

**South
Australia**
`09:30`

Queensland

Brisbane

**Coolangatta
Tweed Heads**

`11:30`

New South Wales

Broken Hill
`09:30`

**Norfolk
Island**

Perth

Eucla
`08:45`

Adelaide

Sydney

`10:30`

**Lord
Howe
Island**

Victoria
Melbourne

N

1 000 km

Hobart

NEW
ZEALAND

Tasmania

`07:00`   `08:00`   `09:00`   `10:00`   `11:00`   `12:00`

Strange time warps · Australia

*Time zone anomalies so weird you can even celebrate a new year
twice on the same night*

If you do a Google search for the time in Sydney and then in the New South Wales town of Broken Hill (population 17,800), in the same state, you will see the latter is 30 minutes behind the state capital. Unlike the rest of New South Wales, Broken Hill and the surrounding region observes Australian Central Standard Time (Universal Co-ordinated Time, UTC + 9:30), the same time zone used in nearby South Australia.

The reason? In 1892, when the Australian dominions adopted standard time, Broken Hill's only direct rail link was with Adelaide, not Sydney.

Similarly, Broken Hill is regarded as part of South Australia for the purposes of postal parcel rates and telephone charges.

Broken Hill also used to be a break-of-gauge station, where the state railway systems of South Australia and New South Wales met.

In its colonial days (until 1899), South Australia was on a central time zone – an hour behind the East. Under pressure from the chamber of commerce to adopt Eastern Standard Time (EST), the government came up with a compromise that put clocks 30 minutes behind those on Australia's eastern seaboard.

Australia's Northern Territory (population 250,000) does not use daylight saving and remains on the same time standard all year.

Lord Howe Island (population 382, part of the Unincorporated Area of New South Wales) uses an offset of UTC + 11 during the summer. In the winter, after daylight saving is over, they set the clocks back half an hour (UTC + 10:30).

Norfolk Island (population 2,169) recently changed from + 11:30 to + 11:00.

The Cocos (Keeling) Islands (population 596), a remote territory of Australia in the Indian Ocean, uses UTC + 6:30.

The official time in the tiny town of Eucla, South Australia (population 53), and the surrounding area is 45 minutes ahead of Western Australia (WA) and 45 minutes behind South Australia (SA). This is because when Eucla was founded in 1885, the time difference between SA and WA was an hour and 30 minutes, so it was decided to set a time there halfway between WA time and SA time, which gave birth to a new time zone of 45 minutes.

The town of Tweed Heads (population 8,200), at the very north of New South Wales, merges seamlessly into Coolangatta (population just under 6,000) on Queensland's Gold Coast. The two states are ostensibly in the same time zone, but New South Wales observes daylight saving, and Queensland does not. That means the twin towns have managed to carve out a peculiar niche as somewhere you can celebrate New Year's Eve twice. Start in Tweed Heads, then stroll to Coolangatta, where the party starts again an hour later.

ABOUT JONGLEZ PUBLISHING

It was September 1995 and Thomas Jonglez was in Peshawar, the northern Pakistani city 20 kilometres from the tribal zone he was to visit a few days later. It occurred to him that he should record the hidden aspects of his native city, Paris, which he knew so well. During his seven-month trip back home from Beijing, the countries he crossed took in Tibet (entering clandestinely, hidden under blankets in an overnight bus), Iran and Kurdistan. He never took a plane but travelled by boat, train or bus, hitch-hiking, cycling, on horseback or on foot, reaching Paris just in time to celebrate Christmas with the family.

On his return, he spent two fantastic years wandering the streets of the capital to gather material for his first "secret guide", written with a friend. For the next seven years he worked in the steel industry until the passion for discovery overtook him. He launched Jonglez Publishing in 2003 and moved to Venice three years later.

In 2013, in search of new adventures, the family left Venice and spent six months travelling to Brazil, via North Korea, Micronesia, the Solomon Islands, Easter Island, Peru and Bolivia. After seven years in Rio de Janeiro, he now lives in Berlin with his wife and three children.

Jonglez Publishing produces a range of titles in nine languages, released in 40 countries.

ABOUT THE AUTHOR

© Christine Bohling

Vitali Vitaliev is a UK-based multi-award-winning author, columnist, editor and broadcaster. Starting his career in the former USSR, where he became known as the country's first investigative journalist, he was forced to defect in January 1990. Having worked and lived in Australia, England, Scotland and Ireland, and having travelled in over 70 countries, Vitali is the author of 15 books translated into many languages. He has worked as a journalist for some of the major English-language newspapers, and is now a Royal Literary Fund Fellow as well as a Writing Fellow and Teaching Associate at the University of Cambridge, but also a Fellow of the Royal Geographical Society of Great Britain. Vitali lives with his partner Christine and Tashi, a furry Tibetan Terrier, in a small English town not far from London.

FROM THE SAME PUBLISHER

Photo Books

Abandoned America
Abandoned Asylums
Abandoned Australia
Abandoned churches – Unclaimed places of worship
Abandoned cinemas of the world
Abandoned France
Abandoned Italy
Abandoned Japan
Abandoned Lebanon
Abandoned Spain
After the Final Curtain – The Fall of the American Movie Theater
After the Final Curtain – America's Abandoned Theaters
Baikonur – Vestiges of the Soviet Space Programme
Chernobyl's Atomic Legacy
Forbidden Places
Forbidden Places – Vol.2
Forbidden Places – Vol.3
Forgotten Heritage
Oblivion
Unusual wines
Venice deserted
Venice from the skies

"Soul of" Guides

Soul of Athens – A guide to 30 exceptional experiences
Soul of Barcelona – A guide to 30 exceptional experiences
Soul of Berlin – A guide to the 30 best experiences
Soul of Kyoto – A guide to 30 exceptional experiences
Soul of Lisbon – A guide to 30 exceptional experiences
Soul of Los Angeles – A guide to 30 exceptional experiences
Soul of Marrakesh – A guide to 30 exceptional experiences
Soul of New York – A guide to 30 exceptional experiencess
Soul of Rome – A guide to 30 exceptional experiencess
Soul of Tokyo – A guide to 30 exceptional experiences
Soul of Venice – A guide to 30 exceptional experiences

"Secret" Guides

Secret Amsterdam
Secret Bali
Secret Bangkok
Secret Barcelona
Secret Belfast
Secret Berlin
Secret Brighton – An unusual guide
Secret Brooklyn
Secret Brussels
Secret Buenos Aires
Secret Campania
Secret Cape Town
Secret Copenhagen
Secret Dublin – An unusual guide
Secret Edinburgh – An unusual guide
Secret Florence
Secret French Riviera
Secret Geneva
Secret Glasgow
Secret Granada
Secret Helsinki
Secret Istanbul
Secret Johannesburg
Secret Lisbon
Secret Liverpool – An unusual guide
Secret London – An unusual guide
Secret London – Unusual bars & restaurants
Secret Los Angeles
Secret Madrid
Secret Mexico City
Secret Milan
Secret Montreal - An unusual guide
Secret Naples
Secret New Orleans
Secret New York – An unusual guide
Secret New York – Curious activities
Secret New York – Hidden bars & restaurants
Secret Paris
Secret Prague
Secret Provence
Secret Rio
Secret Rome
Secret Seville
Secret Singapore
Secret Sussex – An unusual guide
Secret Tokyo
Secret Tuscany
Secret Venice
Secret Vienna
Secret York – An unusual guide

Follow us on Facebook, Instagram and Twitter